THE WALL STREET DIET

THE WALL STREET DIET

MAKING YOUR BUSINESS LEAN AND HEALTHY

CHARLES C. POIRIER

MICHAEL J. BAUER

WILLIAM F. HOUSER

BERRETT-KOEHLER PUBLISHERS, INC.
San Francisco

Berrett-Koehler Publishers, Inc.
235 Montgomery Street, Suite 650
San Francisco, CA 94104-2916
Tel: (415) 288-0260   Fax: (415) 362-2512   www.bkconnection.com

Ordering Information

Quantity sales. Special discounts are available on quantity purchases by corporations,
associations, and others. For details, contact the "Special Sales Department" at the
Berrett-Koehler address above.

Individual sales. Berrett-Koehler publications are available through most bookstores.
They can also be ordered directly from Berrett-Koehler: Tel: (800) 929-2929;
Fax: (802) 864-7626; www.bkconnection.com

Orders for college textbook/course adoption use. Please contact Berrett-Koehler:
Tel: (800) 929-2929; Fax: (802) 864-7626.

Orders by U.S. trade bookstores and wholesalers. Please contact Publishers Group
West, 1700 Fourth Street, Berkeley, CA 94710. Tel: (510) 528-1444; Fax (510) 528-3444.

Production management: Michael Bass Associates

Berrett-Koehler and the BK logo are registered trademarks of Berrett-Koehler
Publishers, Inc.

Printed in the United States of America

Berrett-Koehler books are printed on long-lasting acid-free paper. When it is available,
we choose paper that has been manufactured by environmentally responsible processes.
These may include using trees grown in sustainable forests, incorporating recycled paper,
minimizing chlorine in bleaching, or recycling the energy produced at the paper mill.

Library of Congress Cataloging-in-Publication Data
Poirier, Charles C., 1936–
   The Wall Street diet: making your business lean and healthy /
by Charles C. Poirier, Michael J. Bauer, and William F. Houser.
    p. cm.
  Includes bibliographical references and index.
  ISBN-10: 1-57675-381-6; ISBN-13: 978-1-57675-381-1
   1. Organizational change. 2. Reengineering (Management)
3. Industrial management. 4. Industrial efficiency. I. Bauer, Michael J., 1947–
II. Houser, William F., 1940– III. Title.
  HD58.8.P65 2006
  658.4'063--dc22

2005055599

First Edition
11 10 09 08 07 06   10 9 8 7 6 5 4 3 2 1

*Charles Poirier—For all the friends and associates
who contributed ideas and thoughts*

*Michael Bauer—I have to acknowledge the impact of the
Beaumont Hospital Weight Loss program in Troy, Michigan,
for making me understand the benefits of a change in lifestyle,
not in diet, that makes improving your health the bottom line,
not weight loss. In addition, the support of the world-class team
at the Mayo Clinic Executive Health Program in Rochester, Minnesota,
and in particular Dr. Deborah Rhodes for her encouragement
and assistance in maintaining a healthy lifestyle.
The lessons learned about achieving better health had a direct impact
on the Wall Street Diet and the view that you have to change
your lifestyle, both personal and business, to achieve lasting benefit.
Of course, without the help and support of my wife Karen,
none of this would be possible.*

*William Houser—For all of the great relationships
that made this book possible*

CONTENTS

PREFACE

A diet book for business?

Yes, *The Wall Street Diet* is a book about improving the health of a business. The Wall Street Diet is not a fad diet. It is much more. It concentrates on improving business health and wealth through diagnosis and a comprehensive program to prepare the enterprise for tomorrow.

The Wall Street Diet is based on the same principles that a successful human dieter has to adopt. The successful dieter focuses on adopting a new lifestyle to attain not just weight loss but improved health. Countless studies have shown dieters constantly lose weight, only to regain it repeatedly. Successful dieters improve their health and make it last.

Why the Wall Street Diet? The results will give you the financial and market success that will provide long-term benefits for the investment community, your shareholders, and your employees.

What can you expect from the Wall Street Diet? First, just as a successful dieter should, you should start with a comprehensive "physical" or, in diet terms, a diagnostic, so you can understand exactly where your firm is and what steps you should take immediately. We'll show you how to find hidden profits. Second, we will describe how to determine your business's next steps and activities; this is the "diet" plan. Third, we will show you the actual diet—how many calories; which, if any, medications; the exercise program; tips on the percentage of fat, cholesterol, and so forth. Those hidden profits will now be on the bottom line. In this diet, it is all about optimizing your supply chain, making yourself lean, custom-designing quality programs, collaborating, and focusing on the customer.

A successful dieter relies on a doctor's advice, changes his or her lifestyle, diets, and exercises (Exhibit FM.1). For a business, the approach is very similar (Exhibit FM.2).

EXHIBIT FM.1 Successful Dieting.

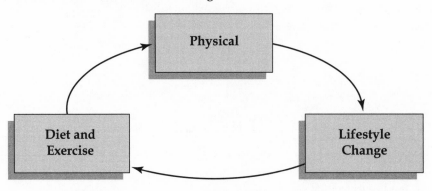

EXHIBIT FM.2 Wall Street Diet Process.

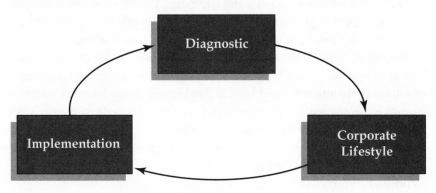

Do a company-wide diagnosis of everything. Choose a new lifestyle or thorough business strategy. Implement. Then repeat for greater advantage.

Your firm may have adopted a significant program around quality, lean manufacturing, or some other improvement methodology. Unfortunately, these efforts by themselves will probably not be sufficient to give you a competitive edge. Is lean bad? Is quality bad? No, it is just that a massive body of evidence indicates that they are not enough, and over time they lose their edge and do not become part of a corporate lifestyle. They become programs with diminishing returns. Our goal is to provide you with the tools and techniques of the diet to cause lasting change.

The genesis of this diet occurred when one of the authors lost more than fifty pounds by adopting a lifestyle change including low-fat foods, regular exercise, and constant attention to health metrics: cholesterol, blood pressure, heart rate, weight, and so forth. The effort was successful and sustainable by the change in lifestyle, not a fad diet.

We compared the current situation in the business world with the current situation in consumer dieting—countless new programs or diets, limited success, then a need to start over again, often in a worse position than before.

We noticed in marked contrast that a person facing a life-threatening health condition or a person determined to maintain a healthy lifestyle will quickly accept substantial changes. This approach is fundamentally different from adopting a fad diet. The successful dieters focus on overcoming chronic health problems or sustaining good health, not the desire to be slimmer. They are the exceptions.

When we look at the business landscape, we see similar patterns. Businesses move from fad to fad, but they soon fall into old patterns without really changing. Businesses follow crash programs to cover failed business processes. Most of the time, though, it's business as usual. For all the articles, books, courses, new ideas, and improvement techniques, businesses still struggle to achieve lasting business greatness.

We also noticed that successful businesses facing crises in either financial health or survival of the enterprise can overcome chronic problems. These businesses will react quickly when they find the market now demands lower costs, higher quality, quicker responses, or shorter cycle times. They, too, are the exceptions.

We developed the Wall Street Diet because we know that the same principles that make an individual healthy can be directly applied to a business.

The Wall Street Diet takes an easily understood metaphor—the diet—and applies it to business operations. To make an individual healthy for the long run, lifestyle changes must be made. Businesses are no different; they also need to make lifestyle changes.

The Wall Street Diet is easy to communicate. Shareholders, employees, customers, suppliers—everyone—will be able to understand and identify with your new regimen. Engaging individuals is a key component of the diet.

The Wall Street Diet is a way to better business health without cutting back on human resources, a way to transform underachievers into overachievers, a way based on action, not excuses, and a way to lasting success.

We have an exciting vision of what the Wall Street Diet can do. After adopting the diet, the firm and a few of its carefully selected business partners create a new kind of enterprise. It has no stovepipes, which cripple improvement efforts, or the departmental anarchy that inhibits sharing valuable knowledge. It is highly collaborative. There is no waste. All processes add value. The firm is also positioned better against its competitors to meet unexpected changes in the marketplace.

Our research also shows that senior management commitment and involvement are critical. Delegation and participation are crucial elements, to be sure, but the perspective and vision from the top are essential. If senior management is not actively engaged, the chances of success go down.

If senior management is committed, and the approach is comprehensive, the results are dramatic. We discovered senior management will always appreciate the five to eight points of new profit to the bottom line. And that's year after year. Your business can become permanently more profitable.

This book begins where others leave off. *The Wall Street Diet* provides a prescriptive, balanced guide to a higher ground in business performance, applying a contemporary business model.

There are no shortcuts. We will warn you up-front that there is hard work. We are changing lifestyles. We believe that the results more than justify the means.

The Wall Street Diet will make you the industry leader. And the overall goal is sustainability. When you change your business lifestyle, you will gain strength and endurance and live longer, profitably.

ACKNOWLEDGMENTS

The individuals who were most helpful in contributing to this book are cited as the material and case studies are presented. Special thanks must be given to Alex Black, Brad Barton, Brad Bush, Simon Buesnel, Ben Cagle, Steve Caulkins, Chet Chetzron, Martin Collard, Jeremy Davies, Alan Free, Drew Gant, Steve Goble, Janet Herin, Jane Howell, Marty Jacobsen, Gary Jones, Larry Lapide, Bill Mees, Steve Miller, Steve Simco, Bud Wagner, Ian Walker, and Timothy Zullo. The enthusiastic encouragement and advice provided by our publisher, Steven Piersanti, and his excellent staff were also critical elements in producing this book. Special thanks go to the editors who helped bring the text into presentable form, including Jeffrey Kulick, Alis Valencia, and Bill Ralph. Jeff took special time to bring the format into a reader-friendly version, and we particularly appreciate his assistance.

will inspire alignment and commitment to stretch objectives. The Wall Street Diet is that plan. This diet requires implementing the lean productivity and quality aspects needed to lead an industry and combining them with features of selective outsourcing and advanced supply chain management principles across a trusting business network. The objective is to achieve the greatest return on investments in capital assets, human resources, collective skills, and enterprise knowledge. It means integrating the messages from the Wall Street Diet into a process for finding total enterprise optimization, and using the benefits to build new revenues, so the end result is a dramatic improvement to enterprise profits, no matter the current state of earnings.

CHECKLIST FOR SENIOR MANAGEMENT

☐ Use the Wall Street Diet as a device to communicate clearly both your plans and the enterprise's needs to all constituents.

☐ Make certain all parts of your organization are subjected to the analysis that goes with the diet. Improvement opportunities can occur in the most unlikely places.

CHECKLIST FOR FUNCTIONAL MANAGERS AND DIET CHAMPIONS

☐ Understand how the diet metaphor affects you and your team. Use it to communicate clearly your desire for optimized conditions.

☐ Understand the actions you have to take to make your company successful.

START YOUR DIET—CREATE A LEAN ENTERPRISE

When a person decides to go on a diet, there are ways to increase the chances of success. The dieter must change a lifetime of accumulated bad habits in eating and adopt a new lifestyle to develop more desirable body conditions.

The secrets for a business are to keep in sync with changing market conditions and always be the best in an industry. Underlying both scenarios is the ability to change old habits and adapt to new environments.

Losing weight requires a change in eating habits. Building a lean enterprise requires a change in business habits. A lean business enterprise requires less working capital and fewer resources.

Just as a human dieter uses different recipes or looks for alternatives on the menu, the business will also require different recipes and menu selections. A business must use its quality program in a similar manner to ensure the firm and its business allies always operate at peak performance without facing the same old problems.

Exercise is also a necessary ingredient in keeping the weight from coming back, which is accomplished as the individual burns additional calories. A business follows a similar path by generating continual process improvements.

The individual's changed lifestyle stays under control by having partners who offer support, while the business makes better choices of its business allies and uses their help to enhance the linked processes.

Our goal with the Wall Street Diet is to draw on these similarities, to help anyone in any type of company to produce a healthier business as part of a leaner enterprise. Health for the business requires substantial changes to current activities, just as an individual makes changes in lifestyle. A robust business must also adopt a better set of business practices that sustain the firm now and in the future. Companies as well as individuals must change behavior.

The Wall Street Diet is about putting everything together in one improvement discipline and developing long-term sustainable advantages. In effect, the Wall Street Diet is about changing the culture that drives the operating processes of the business. The objective is improving a firm's financial and competitive posture, by measuring the effect of the changes from a Wall Street perspective—better earnings, growth, continuous improvement and the greatest value for all pertinent stakeholders.

THE WALL STREET DIET ILLUSTRATED

Exhibit 2.1 describes the ingredients of the Wall Street Diet—a framework for the future or contemporary business model. The single-business perspective focuses on both costs and revenues. This framework also provides the structure for this book.

On the cost side, the firm begins by taking advantage of its efforts with advanced supply chain management (ASCM), to be described in Chapter 3. ASCM focuses on achieving best practices across end-to-end business processing, and achieving unprecedented capabilities in product and service flow, cycle times, inventory management, and delivery capability. Examples will be used to show how a number of firms have become industry leaders through application of ASCM.

Lean manufacturing (Chapter 4) is added next, with its emphasis on using people to find and eradicate the root causes of problems and to eliminate all waste within a business. Applying lean ideas to a business enterprise extends that concept beyond the walls of a single company to customers, distributors, and suppliers. Companies frequently make a mistake by confining "lean" to a factory environment. The Wall Street Diet corrects that bad habit. A lean enterprise goes beyond the shop floor, the warehouse, or shipping dock into the office, administrative functions, services, and overhead processes; it goes across the end-to-end supply chain. In that sense, attention is brought to all functions and processes with an eye to making them lean or free of all waste. Toyota has applied lean across its total processing and has a commanding lead in its industry. We will use examples from that firm throughout the text.

There is a way to change your lifestyle, to get rid of the fat and tighten up your bottom line.

Consider a man or woman changing his or her lifestyle. Clogged arteries are life threatening. A business improves its processes throughout its supply chain to ensure nothing is clogging its circulation.

Achieving lower weight requires fewer calories. Creating a lean business enterprise means the business absorbs less in the form of working capital and resources.

A human dieter learns to cut back on high-calorie foods and eats a healthier diet. A business must use quality imperatives in a similar manner to ensure the firm and its business allies always operate at peak performance.

Exercise is also a necessary ingredient in keeping the weight from coming back, as the individual burns calories. A business follows a similar path by generating continual process improvements.

The individual has changed his or her lifestyle encouraged by partners who offer support. Similarly, the business makes better choices of its business allies and uses their help to enhance the linked processes.

The Wall Street Diet is about putting everything together in one improvement discipline and developing long-term sustainable advantages. In effect, it is about changing the culture that drives the business's operating processes. The objective becomes improving a firm's financial and competitive posture by measuring the effect of the changes from a Wall Street perspective—better earnings, growth, continuous improvement, and the greatest value for all stakeholders.

Like a truly effective weight loss program, the Wall Street Diet is a plan for achieving sustained benefits—not in the typical thirty-, sixty-, or ninety-day cycle that catches the attention of the short-term analyst. The diet is designed to appeal to professional Wall Street investors. They will want to see a long-term plan and regular measurements, exactly as a physician would evaluate a patient. Exactly what the Wall Street Diet prescribes.

Building peak and lasting performance in terms of cost, productivity, and quality is the greatest challenge facing organizations today. Odds are your firm has probably been through a number of change initiatives. Many employees and analysts just roll their eyes when you announce another. The results may have temporarily strengthened the firm or parts of it, but has there been substantial impact on the bottom line?

Fundamental improvements that endure require fundamental changes to the business. The will to improve is not enough. Tools and integrated approaches are necessary to achieve a lean and fit organization.

In the end, the enterprise is characterized by what we call *full network connectivity*, linking all partners in a passion to dominate markets. The companies forming this new network share knowledge and establish the communications links to transfer vital information on supplies, inventories, goods in transit, warehouse stocks, and so forth. Using technology is essential. You will have a network with the lowest total cost. Leading firms have these objectives as targets. You should as well, and we will show you how. We want you to build a company that is as healthy in fifty years as it is in five.

In addition to the five to eight points of potential new profit to the bottom line, your firm will also see benefits to planning, order management and processing, order-to-cash cycle times, just-in-time deliveries, and inventory management. The healthier firm focuses on greater customer satisfaction, so achievements should also be made to on-time deliveries, fill rates, returns, and other measures important to the customer.

The firm discovers the emerging enterprise has more than new skills; it has knowledge that can be leveraged in the marketplace, especially to better satisfy customers. Firms that embrace the concepts inherent in the Wall Street Diet have used such ability to open a serious gap between them and less able competitors, with several companies beginning to dominate their industries.

KEY CONCEPTS

Like other diet programs, the Wall Street Diet introduces concepts that ask the dieter to support changing his or her lifestyle. While these concepts are developed in later chapters, we want you to get a better sense here of what the diet is all about.

One concept is *total enterprise optimization*, or TEO. This is the healthy and profitable result of integrating four ingredients for cost improvement: advanced supply chain management, lean manufacturing, quality, and selective outsourcing. These four are applied to both your firm and its closest allies.

Another concept is the idea of *value-managed enterprise*. The enterprise will be transformed by four ingredients to generate revenue increases: benefits derived from advanced supply chain management, customer intelligence, customer relationship management, and technology collaboration. These factors appeal to desired customers and will generate higher sales and revenues. By infusing a balanced diet across its total processing system, this enterprise will dominate its industry in the present and for as long as the changed lifestyle adapts to changing market constraints.

In using the terms *optimized* and *optimization*, in essence we are referring to the point where further improvements in the process or system would cost more than their benefits. We are looking for the point that yields the greatest result without adding costs.

Another key concept is the new idea of a federated *keiretsu*—a loosely coupled network of businesses working toward common purposes. We propose a less formal structure than is traditionally part of this concept, as well as profound new ways to share information and the work to be done. The Wall Street Diet creates improved processes beyond the four walls of the firm with the help of trusted business partners.

Our message is basic: Put your company on a diet, with the help of key business allies, and keep the gains you make to establish an advantage over fatter, less healthy competitors. This strategy is the result of twenty-first-century business reality, not twentieth-century business mythology. In this arrangement, all parties will be lean and add value at each point of interaction across the value-managed enterprise.

INTEGRATING KEY CONCEPTS

A central theme in the Wall Street Diet is using the supply chain to build improvements across a wide view of the enterprise. Health and financial well-being for the firm will never be achieved without rigorous analysis to determine that it has the best operating techniques, quality, and costs at each link in its end-to-end supply chain system. Where deficiencies are noted, a diet-enhancing ingredient must be applied.

Another central theme in the Wall Street Diet is an emphasis on using lean techniques or getting rid of the fat anywhere in the business enterprise. We see a renewal in the appreciation of lean techniques as a way to eliminate all waste within a total business operating system. It is absolutely essential to apply the principles not in a vacuum but with other ingredients of our diet in a balanced manner—across extended enterprises in a coordinated effort to reduce all wastes. As firms move forward with what is becoming global attention to supply chain management, for example, there is a definite need to harmonize those efforts with lean techniques, while following a quality prescription that ensures root causes of problems are eliminated, the improvements tracked, and the benefits sustained.

Selective outsourcing should be used carefully in this effort to move certain processes into the hands of your most capable and trusted external business allies. These network partners simply have better processes. There is no reason for your firm to operate with worse tools or processes. We will explain in detail and through the help of supporting case material exactly how industry leaders are carrying out such an effort.

We will also demonstrate that revenue growth must be approached with the same rigor as the pursuit of total least cost, also across the business network. By taking advantage of the improvements gained through its drive for TEO, a firm will have shorter cycle times, greater transparency in its supply network operations, better matching of demand with supply, and unprecedented reliability in its processing. You will see how the benefits gained through advanced supply chain management are used in conjunction with better customer intelligence and customer relationship management to differentiate the business network in the eyes of the most desired customers. You will use technology as a key enabler to execute this part of the Wall Street Diet, yielding new profits and revenues.

The Wall Street Diet can add five to eight points of new profit.

THE HARD REALITIES

We have worked with many firms and individuals to introduce the Wall Street Diet and its key elements, and we have noticed it is far easier to grasp parts of it than the whole. We have also found almost universal reactions.

First, CEOs and senior managers understand the individual disciplines. They have been through, or at least know about, quality management, lean manufacturing, and other business improvement approaches. These individual approaches are part of their management tool kit. The Wall Street Diet demonstrates how to *combine and leverage* these approaches for greatest impact.

Second, younger managers are not as familiar with these intangible approaches, but they almost innately understand the technology aspects.

The diet can succeed only when these two perspectives are merged, when partnering occurs across generations within an enterprise. It's not just about the techniques; it's not just about technology.

At the end of each chapter are checklists to help you determine the next steps in pursuing the Wall Street Diet. You will find suggestions for senior management, who have broad perspectives and special concerns, and also for functional/business unit managers and diet champions, whose focus tends more toward implementation.

The diet will challenge many of the tried-and-true assumptions about the structure of organizations and relations with suppliers and customers. We know something about your firm—the profits are there and need to be released. Just as the successful dieter maintains an image of a healthier individual, you will uncover a more profitable and healthy firm.

The Wall Street Diet is not easy. Sustained effort across the firm and beyond will be required. We recognize the cultural issues and the concerns that will be raised.

Successful dieters understand that changing lifestyles is the key. And, changing a lifestyle is not easy. The results, however, more than justify abandoning the unhealthy, minimally profitable current state.

The Wall Street Diet will help readers understand how assimilating the "business diet," attractive to Wall Street and designed for long-term improvement, can add value for any firm of any size in any business. Your firm will achieve the greatest return on effort. You will include your business network constituents, including investors, suppliers, business customers, and consumer groups. You will have a methodology for calibrating and tracking sustainable success. With many case examples and action stories, we bring a new and higher dimension to business success by explaining how to select trusted business allies, with whom critical business knowledge is shared for mutual benefit.

The objective is the creation of a truly linked and optimized business network or value-managed enterprise, where the member companies are working together with a contemporary business model that delivers greater value than any competing network.

CONTEMPORARY BUSINESS MODELS

Leading firms have done more than bring a new dimension to supply chain, lean, and quality management. They have begun to implement a series of principles and techniques to hold the gains while they continue finding further improvements. These firms are not standing still. They are applying the contemporary model to gain distinctive advantages and market leads. The key is to target what will become the best future practices and apply the Wall Street Diet to achieve and hold such a position.

The Wall Street Diet model creates a sustainable competitive advantage. Competitors may imitate a part of your success, but the long-term value resides in the complete system. Some years ago, companies launched projects to emulate certain world-class manufacturers, particularly Toyota. This automaker had extended the concept of lean beyond its manufacturing system to encompass its entire supply chain. The result was a closely coupled keiretsu, or value network, that is profitable at every link. Toyota is a great example of a successful business dieter and what we have termed the value-managed enterprise. Why does Toyota allow nearly anyone to tour its plants and look at its processes? Because the Toyota lifestyle is the real advantage, not just the Toyota production system.

Many of the would-be Toyota imitators were able to point to their temporary reductions in factory inventory, neater work areas, more streamlined processing, and fewer mistakes, but they failed in the long run to hold the gains. In particular, we saw the auto industry touting just-in-time inventory. We think they really meant "just-not-here" inventory. Unfortunately for these companies, within a short time, warehouses bulged with unnecessary inventories, rework and returns came back, and blame was laid at the feet of suppliers and workers for poor quality.

Industry leaders such as Toyota, Wal-Mart, IBM, Dell, Nike, Tesco, Procter & Gamble, and Intel forsake business fads. They capitalize on the benefits achieved through their long-term drive beyond the four walls of their enterprise, focusing on bottom- and top-line performance—a contemporary business model. The model applies a combined effort to focus on the top line (sales and revenues) as well as the bottom line (costs and efficiencies) to nearly double or triple earnings. This new system has application to all industries, including the service sector.

SUMMARY

Achieving and holding a position of leadership in an industry by virtue of having the healthiest business lifestyle requires a clear plan—a viable and well-understood vision of how a changed state of business performance

CHANGE YOUR LIFESTYLE—
INTRODUCE THE WALL STREET DIET

A business diet? Is this just another plan to cut more jobs, reduce more facilities, or sell a portion of the business? Nothing could be further from the truth. Our goal is to provide practical steps to build a stronger, healthier company whose profit and loss statement will show five to eight points of new profit on the bottom line. The diet will transform the organization and extend to the most important business allies—suppliers, distributors, customers, and everyone in the supply chain.

If the objective for the individual is the best in good health, then the objective in the business world would be the best operating conditions across the end-to-end supply chain—in essence, a lean enterprise. If the individual wants to attain improved health, the business wants to sustain gains made through enhanced financial statements. Drawing on these similarities, we can see that individuals and businesses have some common goals, as described in the accompanying chart.

Why is it the Wall Street Diet? We've added a Wall Street–inspired framework to the health diet metaphor that will work in virtually any kind of business in any industry. We match the human diet ingredients with the necessary business characteristics from the view of the Wall Street investor. This framework has two themes: first, make lasting improvements to the cost structure of a business; second, use the benefits of those improvements to generate new revenues.

People, not unlike businesses, often make the mistake of moving from one improvement fad to another, in hopes of weight loss or enhancement of appearance. Overall, however, the average person's weight keeps climbing, and the related health problems increase. Drawn to the diet du jour, overweight people try various diets to bring their weights down, and

Individuals	Businesses
Low blood pressure and heart rate	Unobstructed supply chain flows, improved processing, and best cycle times
Healthy food intake	
Nutritional diet	Collaborative suppliers and distributors
Correct weight (Body Mass Index [BMI])	Collaborative business partners
Weight loss	Lean manufacturing techniques—lowest total costs
Proper ratio of high-density lipoprotein (HDL) to low-density lipoprotein (LDL)	Balanced supply and demand characteristics, without excess inventory
New recipes and menus	New quality and lean tool kits
Annual physical examinations	Quality improvement and standards
Working with the doctor to recalibrate ideal results; undergoing tests and measurements	Productivity profiling
	Strengthening the network through selective outsourcing
Building support systems	Total enterprise best practices
Workout regimen	Cultural change and increased profit
New lifestyle with healthy eating habits	Flexibility, agility, and responsiveness
High energy	
Strength	Strong earnings
Healthier, more attractive body	Healthier, more profitable enterprise, more attractive to Wall Street

often they succeed in temporary weight loss. As progress is made, however, sustaining the improvements becomes a real challenge, and quite often dieters try new regimens when they fall back into old habits and regain the lost weight. In a never-ending sequence, the body slims, fattens, and slims again. This scenario is also played, metaphorically, over and over by a large number of modern businesses.

EXHIBIT 2.1   The Business Diet—Framework for the Future

Costs	Revenues

• Lean Manufacturing plus
• Selective Outsourcing plus
• Quality
  — Six Sigma
  — ISO Capability, plus
• Advanced Supply Chain Management
• Yields Total Enterprise Optimization
	• Advanced Supply Chain Management plus
	• Customer Relationship Management plus
	• Technology Collaboration yields
	• Customer Intelligence, which becomes the heart of
	• The Intelligent Value Network

The next ingredient is quality (Chapter 5). The modern perspective stresses appropriate quality standards that are applied to the business conditions. Six Sigma, often touted as the beacon here, has proven to be a beneficial effort for many Wall Street Diet followers. For some organizations, it can be an elusive target and too costly for recovery in the market. One of the unique and most critical features of the Wall Street Diet is its focus on the entire network that forms a business enterprise. While Six Sigma may be a stretch for some organizations, business allies often can provide the help needed to achieve the desired benefit. You can utilize their Six Sigma or other quality capabilities to gain process improvements and keep costs reasonable. You can introduce some of their techniques into your processing. Several examples will be used to describe how this ingredient is applied not only to find new savings but to hold the gains.

Is your business at a theoretical utopian or best possible state? If not, how can you identify specifically what gains are possible? Chapter 6 will provide a special profiling tool to help firms determine just how far off optimized conditions their activities might be and how much improvement is possible.

Just as the human dieter needs support from close friends to stay on the changed regimen, so a business needs external support to reach the conditions of best health. Selective outsourcing (Chapter 7) is used to determine whether the firm is really the best at completing each required process step. One or more steps might be performed better by another business partner. This is a difficult ingredient in the diet but one that is increasingly part of the business arsenal. Leading firms have discovered they can acquire part of their products or services from other suppliers at substantial savings. Boeing is doing precisely that as it farms out most of its new 7E7 Dreamliner airplane to external business contractor/partners.

The Wall Street Diet is much like following the ingredients in a recipe, a formula for business success, or a medical prescription. All are aids to achieving and holding improved health conditions. On the cost side, companies making greater progress are combining lean manufacturing techniques with selective outsourcing, ASCM, and superior quality into a single focus on total enterprise optimization (TEO), with superior customer service becoming a logical by-product of the effort. To address the firm's concerns about such a rigorous diet, we will clearly establish just what TEO benefits might be achieved.

On the revenue side, the Wall Street Diet emphasizes a focus on the most desirable customers (detailed in Chapter 8). This approach is supported by two main elements. First, the ASCM that was developed earlier includes seeing the total process and having very flexible and responsive capabilities. It is combined with customer relationship management (CRM). The secret is to use CRM not as a means to reduce sales costs or foist a strong discipline on sales personnel with little return on the effort. Instead, it should be positioned as a method of applying customer intelligence and technology collaboration to discover, analyze, and develop the appropriate response to actual demand. That means matching supply at the point of need with the demand better than any competing network.

At the core of this part of the effort is *customer intelligence*, which we define as the acquisition, management, and integration of customer knowledge in order to create a differentiating customer value proposition. This intelligence becomes the secret ingredient in the formula. Business partners work together to analyze the enormous amount of data available today on trends and market conditions, customer actions and reactions, and so forth. The result is the correct marketing strategy, taking advantage of the benefits gained from following the prescribed diet. It is called the *value-managed enterprise*, the new business objective where value is added at each link in the processing with customer satisfaction and service as the differentiating factors. With the advantages gained, the enterprise focuses simultaneously on both the bottom line (cost improvement) and the top line (revenue improvement).

COLLABORATIVE EFFORTS ACROSS THE ENTERPRISE THAT SATISFY THE CUSTOMER BECOME THE REAL OBJECTIVE

The Wall Street Diet demands that you bring attention to all facets of the business—lose weight (use less inventory to meet customer demand), have a diet rich in fiber and nutrients (create greater inventory turns for higher revenues), reduce bad cholesterol (build a frictionless supply chain), and exercise regularly (collaborate with business partners to continuously find best practices). But the Wall Street Diet is not just about weight loss; in fact, if you improve your physical condition enough, you may weigh more as you build increased muscle mass. It is about improving the health of your business and the capability of your supply chain. The Wall Street Diet is about changing the way the firm does its business, just as successful dieters change their lifestyles. And there must be a central objective behind the effort—to establish the lean enterprise and, through its processing, to satisfy the intended customer better than any competing business system.

Collaboration becomes a key factor, the ingredient of the diet that might have the most overall benefit. One of the first steps in collaboration is changing the relationship among all members of the supply chain. How important is that step? An illustration from the automotive industry may shed some light. In May 2005, a survey by Planning Perspectives, Inc. (Birmingham, Michigan), showed ratings of automotive industry manufacturers by their key suppliers (Tierney 2005). The ratings indicated which firms suppliers preferred to work with. In order, the manufacturers were ranked as follows:

1. Toyota
2. Honda
3. Nissan
4. DaimlerChrysler
5. Ford
6. General Motors

A few months later, on August 30, 2005, the *Detroit Free Press* published Harbour Consulting's (Troy, Michigan) report on automaker per-vehicle profitability. The results are shown in the following chart. Is it a coincidence that the most profitable automakers had the best ratings, and the companies with the lowest ratings had fared the worst?

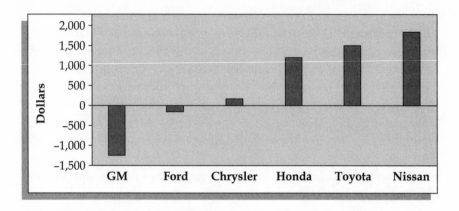

We don't think so. It's a key precept of the Wall Street Diet that in today's connected business world, collaboration is a key differentiator. As a supplier you will bring your best talent, your most creative ideas, and your most innovative approaches to partners whom you can trust and who will value your inputs. Do we mean to imply that the most successful companies do not ask for low prices and high value? No—of course they do, but it's how they go about reducing costs and partnering with suppliers that is key. Toyota is famed for its keiretsu, and we will explain in Chapter 7 how that firm and Honda have gained significant pricing advantages from the same suppliers to those firms at the bottom of the chart. In fact, all three of the most profitable companies have extensive North American operations and work with the same suppliers, yet they achieve remarkably different results.

The Wall Street Diet, therefore, says you must not only manage the internal processes but also extend the improvements to key suppliers, distributors, and customers. The extended enterprise approaches optimized conditions and differentiates itself in the eyes of the customer or important consumer groups. Collaboration with network partners becomes a crucial element in this enterprise optimization, and it should be driven by implementation of the necessary process changes. Exhibit 2.2 illustrates the crucial transition necessary to achieve the objectives being considered—what we term the *N:1 advantage* through the sharing of best skills. It shows that to be successful, a business must leverage the many

EXHIBIT 2.2   The *N:1 Advantage*©—Consolidation Rather Than Linkage

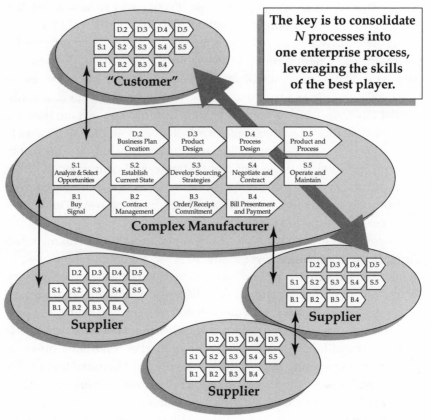

processes across the full enterprise from suppliers to customers. A key part of our diet is to determine which member of the enterprise has the best process techniques at each link in the system. The enterprise then shares them widely. The enterprise view consolidates many suboptimized efforts into single-enterprise processes where possible. The best business partner for each key process is identified, and the process is leveraged throughout the network, which now uses only best practices. For example, if one company has developed the absolutely best method of transacting purchase orders, then that method should be prevalent across what becomes the lean enterprise. Similarly, one order management system with the most effective processing should be in place.

FEDERATED KEIRETSU

The question becomes, What is the most effective way to accomplish this set of optimized conditions and better satisfy the customer? In a broad sense, there are two ways to build effective collaborative enterprises for those purposes. One approach uses the tightly coupled approach—based on the Japanese keiretsu—but with an internal-only focused view that establishes collaboration as a means to gain benefits within a firm's four walls.

For our purposes, we prefer a broader approach, which modifies the standard definition of *keiretsu*, "a network of businesses that own stakes in one another as a means of mutual security, usually including large manufacturers and their suppliers of raw materials and components" (from www.dictionary.com, 2005), to "a network of businesses that are linked electronically and share operating principles, business results and goals, and focus on key market segments."

Toyota provides an example as one of the most successful manufacturing firms in existence. Over many decades, Toyota has developed its tightly coupled keiretsu process to a degree that is has become a very effective business mechanism. This is difficult to emulate because most businesses do not develop such deep-rooted relationships with the supply base and have an aversion to taking ownership positions with suppliers (a characteristic of Japanese keiretsu). Current market conditions, however, present an opportunity to consider another type of keiretsu that fits the Wall Street Diet framework and shows another way to gain many of the benefits of the tightly coupled approach—and do it more quickly. This type of keiretsu will have linked firms with stakes in each other, but not necessarily stock ownership.

*The contemporary value chain moves from
one enterprise driving many processes to
common processes driving many enterprises.*

We refer to this new approach as a *loosely coupled* or *federated keiretsu*. This approach does not have all the benefits of the traditional keiretsu approach, but it has two key benefits: the speed at which it can be implemented and the vastly reduced cost of implementation. A primary reason for these characteristics lies in the fact that most of the physical infrastructure of a federated keiretsu is already in place, but it is not being utilized in an optimal manner. It also is much more easily replicated than the tightly coupled approach.

A major drawback of the federated keiretsu is the complexity of the operating model, involving many constituents and systems of supply and delivery. However, it is still much less complex to operate than the model needed for a traditional keiretsu. The federated keiretsu also does not have the drawbacks of many joint ventures that limit participation in multiple networks and require stock ownership as part of the relationship. The Wall Street Diet recommends a five-point plan to develop an effective federated infrastructure:

1. *Agreement on principles of collaboration*
   It is imperative that companies linked in an enterprise effort develop an operating model, first and foremost, to address areas of profitability objectives, revenue recognition, sourcing responsibilities, employee reporting, compensation and bonus rules, and so forth. It is in effect a jointly developed operating model exactly like an individual company's model. It does not dictate levels of compensation or benefits, but it provides an environment that allows an employee who is engaged in collaborative endeavor to have a seamless interaction throughout the loosely coupled environment of which she or he is now a part. Some key elements will include the following:
   - Shared benefits and rewards through joint process improvements
   - Fusing of many or N core processes in single-enterprise processes, such as planning and warehousing
   - Best-player execution of the processes
   - Integration process teams versus stovepipe teams
   - Unnatural levels of cooperation
   - Coordinated use and application of supporting technologies
   - Multicompany governance to enable radical changes in performance, cycle times, and total enterprise costs
   - New skills and new roles for process owners living in "white space," developing innovative solutions and offerings
   - Organizational neutrality
   - Challenge of the status quo upstream and downstream in the supply chain, with a passion for state-of-the-art processing, practices, skills, and tools

2. *Establishment of a governance model*

The governance model must clearly articulate and define the parameters of intercompany collaboration and employee involvement. It must spell out exactly what will be shared or not shared among the members, what information is sacrosanct, what steps will be taken to ensure security of any shared data, and how best practices will be extended across the enterprise while redundancies in effort will be eliminated.

Many so-called collaborative endeavors have failed to deliver on their promises, primarily because the collaboration has not significantly reduced the time it takes to develop, produce, and support products and services. The problem lies in repetition of processes throughout the supply chain. Each company uses its own processes to develop products and services that are not shared. Employees involved in the change effort, moreover, must use multiple processes, internally and externally.

For example, changes to the design of a product usually entail using all the involved companies' change processes. Instead of multiple processes, the federated keiretsu uses one process, and much of the effort is focused on rationalizing unnecessary processing and choosing the one best approach.

We discuss a specific governance model in both Chapter 4 and Chapter 5 (Exhibits 4.6 and 5.7). The model incorporates all of the issues raised here with specific application to our discussion of lean and quality.

3. *Validation of optimal internal processes*

The quickest way to achieve benefits is the rationalization of processes. That step cannot be accomplished if a company has multiple, sacrosanct processes. Validate the internal processes, and make certain they are consistent and well understood across the network. Do not assume that just because you have adopted a quality process, such as Six Sigma, your process is best in all cases. Search through the processes and functions to find the single best way to arrive at necessary decisions and processes.

For example, if an engineering team, manufacturing team, and support team all have processes and tools designed to cause an engineering change, you have multiple processes that will slow down the firm's activities. If everyone uses a single process to accomplish a single change function, the enterprise moves quickly toward optimized conditions.

4. *Consolidation of processes into the hands of the most capable enterprise member company*
Next, use the single processes across the federated keiretsu. This approach follows the principles of collaboration and the interenterprise governance model. A good rule is to observe organizational neutrality. The best process must be chosen, using accepted benchmarks across industries as indicators to rationalize the processes to be applied.

For example, during the development of a new propulsion unit, several aerospace and defense companies decided to collaborate to meet very tight schedule demands. They quickly determined that using the old methodology would make it impossible to meet these demands. The project team decided to look at each other's core strengths in key areas—product design, program management, metallurgy, and information technology. An honest appraisal showed which company was best in each area, and the tools and processes of the best constituent became the collaborative processes and tools, allowing the consortium to meet the schedule. Where no enterprise member has the best practice at a key process step, an effort should be made to search externally for that knowledge.

5. *Transformation of single constituents into an enterprise*
Transforming the enterprise is the culminating step. The linked companies become entities in the federated keiretsu. The simplest way to achieve this position is to choose your business partners carefully, and then select the market in which you will pursue your initiatives. You will not be successful without business allies, and choosing ones you can trust and work with collaboratively becomes the defining characteristic. In a modern sense, membership in multiple federated keiretsu will make sense, so long as there is an understanding of what is being shared in each entity. That means suppliers may very well participate in multiple value chains with different products and services. The enterprise must, however, have a clear definition of what distinguishing characteristics are featured in its offerings.

RESULTS AT THE TOP AND THE BOTTOM
OF THE PROFIT STATEMENT

Developing the federated keiretsu is a daunting task, but it becomes worthwhile when the benefits are received. The effort is akin to an individual deciding to alter his or her lifestyle with the help of willing supporters. The Wall Street Diet is about improving health and not about shedding resources.

This condition leads us to a modern business paradox that has been emerging for some time now. The mantra for companies during the 1990s was "cost reduction above all else." In spite of the substantial gains many firms made using this approach, over time such a course of action leads to diminishing returns as firms find they can squeeze suppliers and processes only so much, and they often discover they lose the gains after a period of adjustment. Breakthrough technology or heavy capital investments are then needed to reach a higher plateau of improvement. We want firms to achieve higher levels of performance and sustain the new positions without a need to resort to heavy capital investments.

Efforts to improve conditions and satisfy this paradox point to two necessities. First, the business must work diligently at enterprise process improvement, as any weak link in a supply chain can doom the final results. One company cannot be following the Wall Street Diet and driving toward optimized conditions while key suppliers, distributors, and customers are gaining weight. The proper course of action requires a concerted and uniform diet, with a continuous focus on process improvement, being applied across the total value network. Among the industry leaders we see an emerging reliance on carefully selected and trusted business partners to attain such optimized conditions.

Second, technology is an absolute necessity to enable this collaboration, but it must not be presented as the solution. Rather, technology should become the means of providing the knowledge transfer that separates the preferred networks from the wannabes. Technology is the enabler of the improved processing. Our research shows that companies have too often emphasized technology instead of governance and process improvement. It may well be that since technology has common standards, it is easier than developing a uniform governance model and consolidating processes. Technology alone may be easier, but the benefits are miniscule compared to what is possible through optimized processing. Technology should be at the center of knowledge sharing among the enterprise participants.

When these conditions are met, the enterprise can improve the bottom line, through sustained and optimized productivity and cost containment, and the top line, by using the benefits of the enterprise solutions to differentiate itself in the eyes of the most valued customers and end consumers. Attaining this dual capability has been eluding most businesses for some time, as the insatiable desire to reduce costs per se has driven the business focus away from the customer, a fatal mistake. Indeed, our recent research has shown that in spite of the tremendous rhetoric surrounding the importance of the customer as a business driver, the metrics and pay-offs supporting that theme are not present in most businesses. We suggest that, as a result, control of the best customers is up for grabs!

Look no further than the U.S. automobile industry to illustrate our point. The market in both North America and Europe continues to grow, and the new products coming from Asia are ready to explode into these markets. Yet the old paradigms of the U.S. auto industry are prevalent. Companies continue to build plant capacity and force unwarranted cost reductions on an already-compliant supplier base. In the process, they have relegated the customer focus to a back burner. As we will point out in Chapter 7, recent analyses show that key suppliers prefer to work with the Japanese auto manufacturers because they have adopted a more collaborative and less confrontational style.

RETURN ON EFFORT IS SIGNIFICANT

As mentioned in Chapter 1, our research reveals that the return from an effort following the Wall Street Diet can yield five to eight points of new profits for a typical firm and its business allies. Consider first the return on the manufacturing side. Lean concepts will work to eliminate all waste, reduce delay times, and raise productivity. Quality will eliminate the root problems in the processing, reduce costs, and increase efficiency. Backsliding will be banished as the right processing takes place all the time, and systems are not allowed to fail as they are permanently fixed. Selective outsourcing will bring the lowest possible costs and highest efficiency to all process steps. ASCM takes the firm to the highest level of productivity through efforts to find best practices at each process step across the supply chain. With waste and shrinkage at industry-best levels and inventories visible and at the lowest possible levels to meet demand, the firm adds three to five points of new profit, as noted in case studies we have documented.

From the marketing and revenue aspect, the Wall Street Diet is balanced on both sides of the typical business orientation. Supplier management is at work to ensure that the best supply services are present. Product development moves ahead with the help of trusted business partners, as does supply chain management. At the same time, an equal effort is expended on the customer side of the picture, as CRM positively affects sales automation, multichannel customer service, and marketing efforts, all through the use of superior customer intelligence. The TEO capability means out-of-stocks are eliminated. Only the products in demand are produced, so obsolescence ceases. Sales lifts are improved for sales events and special promotions. New revenues are generated with existing and new customers unaccustomed to superior service, often in nontraditional markets.

The network becomes the leader in analyzing and recognizing market trends, and new product and service introductions are completed in industry-best times with a higher rate of success. Pricing is matched with customer needs and willingness to pay for value. Sales and service expenses are reduced and matched to customer segmentation needs. The firm adds another two to three points of new profit. In total, we find the path to a doubling of earnings per share for the shareholders.

THE DIET REQUIRES A SHIFT IN CULTURAL ATTITUDE

Now, finding five to eight points of new profits is extremely important in the current business environment, but it requires compliance to the Wall Street Diet. That means the usual cultural inhibitions restricting the use of external help must be put aside, first internally and then externally (more on this topic in Chapter 9). If the diet is to work, the firm at the center of the business network, or what is often called the *channel master* or *nucleus firm*, must not force its culture and perspectives on the rest of its business partners. There must be a blending and assimilation of what constitutes the right ingredients in the diet and a plan of execution for each constituent with mutual improvement to both costs and revenues.

These statements should not be taken as corporate rhetoric. The combined cultures must reorient the focus to customer service and satisfaction and build backward so the diet can achieve operational excellence and superior customer response. The Wall Street Diet can harmonize supply chain concepts with a stronger commitment to customer expectations and actual requirements. Such a movement strikes at the core of most business cultures, which we have found are far more oriented around internal operational excellence than customer intimacy. The journey toward the improved financial conditions we have described requires a clear vision of the customer or consumer group of choice and an undiluted drive toward differentiating the network from the view of those groups.

The Wall Street Diet brings a new and better dimension to supply chain efforts and the resulting health of the business.

How the Ideal Works

Let's consider the characteristics of our hypothetical but proven contemporary business model, which is a result of rigorously following the Wall Street Diet. The firm becomes a part of creating the best business solutions for the real needs of key customers and consumer groups, matching supply with demand, all derived from its TEO/ASCM efforts. The network introduces customized products and services to meet unique needs faster through a flexible global system. A special range of services is presented, so that customers perceive that they are receiving the most value. In essence, the collaborating firms establish the most responsive system of supply, delivery, and fulfillment.

The benchmarks documenting the differentiating position are also excellent. The management systems are geared toward creating superior results across the end-to-end processing that defines the network. A culture is established that embraces specific rather than general customer service solutions, resulting in strong, lasting relationships built on a new level of trust. Deeper customer knowledge and breakthrough insights are catalogued. Decision making is delegated to employees who make a difference in the eyes of the customers, and these employees take advantage of customer intelligence and visibility across the total network to make promises that are kept. It's a formula for business success, and it becomes the differentiating factor for the future.

Contemporary Business Model

Ping is a familiar name to golfers around the world, a manufacturer of more than a million different custom-designed golf club options. Ping provides twenty thousand pro shops and retailers with those options, delivering most in five days or less. The company also ships custom-manufactured clubs in forty-eight hours or less to golfers who order from one of 2,500 U.S. pro shops that have trained with Ping on custom fittings, a feature not offered by many of its larger competitors. All of this is a result of the firm's build-to-order supply chain, the model of which is based on making products once orders have been received and delivering them in the shortest possible time. Similar to the famous Dell Computer system, the build-to-order concept requires lean manufacturing to eliminate all wastes and delays, or the system simply will not work.

"Our goal is to ship in forty-eight hours," says John Solheim, CEO of the company. "Golfers are usually out on the course on the weekends. If they order a new set of clubs then, the pro shop sends us the order that Monday. What really makes customers happy is they can be playing with their new clubs by the next weekend."

Ping has been advancing toward that goal for some time, beginning with its successful effort to cut the time to bring a new product to market from two years to about nine months. The firm went further by using computer-aided design techniques and "software for managing product life cycles to digitize and manage every aspect of developing golf clubs." Under the new lean system, employees access the company's database via a high-speed Internet system and query the system in real time to find open orders. These orders are grouped based on specifications to "dynamically generate requests for work orders," which are then passed on to the appropriate assembly departments for rapid make-to-order finishing. Ping can issue authority for special orders that need to be finished in less than forty-eight hours, interrupt the manufacturing schedule, and still keep a sensible flow to the overall manufacturing system, with a lot of orders being delivered in twenty-four hours (Bacheldor 2005: 53).

SUMMARY

The human dieter succeeds only by taking a comprehensive approach to change. Diet, exercise, and lifestyle change together. The results—better health and well-being—are dramatic and visible to all. They must, however, be integrated.

The complexities of modern businesses require a focus on operating models and governance. That is another way of saying corporations and their key business allies must follow a rigorous diet, or some part of the network will stand in the way of finding optimized operating conditions and will miss satisfying important customers. To achieve sustainable performance, new approaches are required, and a business transformation with a focus on total dietary excellence is necessary. We have presented the Wall Street Diet as a prescription for finding and keeping excellent conditions across an extended enterprise, so that all constituents can take advantage of key resources and skills, working collaboratively and effectively as they follow the diet. In subsequent chapters, we will dissect the diet, explaining how a strong commitment will bring the desired results and sustain the improvements.

CHECKLIST FOR SENIOR MANAGEMENT

☐ Review the strengths and weaknesses of the existing organization, and prepare a list of the potential areas needing significant improvement. You may want to start with transportation, customer service, and revenue growth.

☐ Have a core group of trusted advisers consider the framework behind the Wall Street Diet, and match the ingredients with the potential improvements for further study and validation.

☐ Establish a potential operating model that redefines profitability objectives, revenue recognition, sourcing responsibilities, employee reporting, compensation and bonus rules, and so forth, based on the federated keiretsu model.

☐ Make a list of potential advisers to form the governance council.

☐ Be prepared to "sell" the idea of the Wall Street Diet to other CEOs among suppliers and customers.

CHECKLIST FOR FUNCTIONAL MANAGERS AND DIET CHAMPIONS

☐ Establish a format for pursuing the diet in an area or two.

☐ Look outside your own organization for personnel with key skills and capabilities who can help implement the diet.

☐ Study the Wall Street Diet. It includes tools and approaches that you will find essential.

☐ Look for opportunities to collaborate with your extended team.

☐ Learn and use standardized enterprise processes.

☐ Understand the goals and rewards structures of your extended team.

3

REDUCE CHOLESTEROL AND INCREASE FLOW—STREAMLINE YOUR BUSINESS

Clogged arteries are a severe medical problem in the United States. When arteries are healthy, they allow blood to flow easily from the heart. In contrast, arteries clogged with fat stiffen and narrow, reducing blood flow to the heart and making the heart work harder and harder until it eventually fails. High levels of "bad" cholesterol are often the culprit.

The circulatory system of an enterprise is its supply chain, which delivers goods and services and links companies together. A supply chain clogged with unnecessary inventory (fat) puts a strain on the entire enterprise. Inflexible supply chains (stiff arteries) are unwieldy, adding to the burden.

In your business, you need to ensure that the right supplies are delivered in the right quantities to the right places at the right time for maximum effectiveness. Most businesses experience some form of blockages or bottlenecks. These eventually lower profits and cause other problems. Think of your distribution channels as blood vessels. You can use supply chain management to remove blockages and promote healthy flows of materials and information.

The Wall Street Diet features advanced supply chain management as a key element for the enterprise. The key to even greater effectiveness—the additional five- to eight-point improvement at the bottom line—means extending advanced supply chain management to partners beyond the traditional boundaries of the organization.

The Wall Street Diet provides tools and metrics that will guarantee a safer and healthier business by measuring inventory reduction, shorter cycle times, lower transportation and warehousing costs, greater customer satisfaction, and so forth. A key element of our tools and metrics is that they are designed for use by suppliers, manufacturers, distributors, customers, and internal functions.

Our dieter gets a quick overview of current health and well-being through a combination of blood work, blood pressure monitoring, and stress tests. Businesses need a comparable easy-to-use performance tool set that takes a snapshot of the current state of activities. These measurements or key performance indicators include inventory as a percentage of revenues, revenues per employee, cost per unit of product, cost per purchase transaction, the day's sales outstanding, and so forth.

TODAY'S AND TOMORROW'S BUSINESS WORLD

Supply chain management can have a significant impact given the state of contemporary business. Historically, supply chains were simple linear arrangements that proceeded from a supplier of raw material through a manufacturer of finished goods to a distributor or retailer for consumption. Those arrangements contained process steps that were not complicated with well-defined costs across the system. Improvement efforts were focused on making value-adding changes to various steps in the processing to reduce costs to the lowest possible levels. For a service business, the flow was similar and might proceed from suppliers of products to a bank, insurance company, or hotelier and through the firm's service personnel to consumers.

Today, these systems are called *supply chains*, and they are becoming complex networks of companies in collaboration with other businesses in an attempt to optimize overall processing. Large corporations operate within supply chain networks as a nucleus firm, driving the processing. Others in the supply chain have important roles. Key suppliers bring designs and necessary components to the process. A distributor or subcontractor takes responsibility for an important process step. In the most advanced networks, all constituents focus on satisfying the most valued customers or consumer groups.

Having a fat partner only weakens the overall effort and endangers the results at the consumption end of the system. Using our diet analogy, all members of a supply chain need to have low cholesterol. Their operations must be free of blockages that slow the flow of goods and services, and create conditions that are not competitive and increase costs.

In other words, every one of the companies in the network must have responsive hearts and arteries that are not clogged or restricted in flow, so that they can react quickly and effectively under stress. The supply chain must be fast and unencumbered, without excess inventory, waste, or non-value-adding administrative tasks. The linked partners should follow a diet high in business substance, providing customers with high-quality goods and services delivered in the right quantities at the right time. The network should absorb the right amount of calories—enough resources to maintain the system like a finely trained athlete but without gaining extra weight or extra costs.

In this chapter, we consider the first element of the Wall Street Diet—advanced supply chain management—to bring all important members of such a chain into a state of lean responsiveness. We employ a five-level supply chain maturity model to explain the route to the highest possible business health. Your firm will need to have its house in order by accomplishing the first two levels of that model. Using the model as part of a business dietary plan will lead any company to improved business results.

Every company in a value chain must focus the results of the leaner conditions on better responsiveness to the customer.

THE FIVE LEVELS OF SUPPLY CHAIN MANAGEMENT

The Wall Street Diet begins within a supply chain, the cardiovascular system of any business enterprise. The major objective is to focus the linked businesses on achieving the highest possible customer and consumer satisfaction. The Wall Street Diet will create superior supply chain conditions to reflect the perfect body or optimized business processing. Procter & Gamble, for example, has made great strides in its pursuit of supply chain, one element of which is the "perfect order," which contains no errors, meets all quality standards, and completely satisfies the customer.

In general terms, a business enterprise evolves through five levels on its way to the most advanced positions of supply chain progress, as illustrated in Exhibit 3.1. We will explore the critical elements of each level.

EXHIBIT 3.1 The Supply Chain Maturity Model

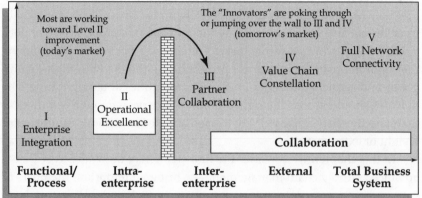

Before embarking on a supply chain effort, typically some other improvement process is already under way, possibly focused on total quality management, business process reengineering, continuous improvement processing, or transportation and logistics. Most firms enhance the benefits from such efforts by carrying forward the better practices to help further improve performance and profits. A firm may already have, for example, the best way to enter and process orders, and it would not be practical to redesign such processing. These best practices can now be merged under an end-to-end umbrella effort that becomes known as *supply chain*. The firm enters the first level of the maturity model.

Level 1—Enterprise Integration

In Level 1, the firm focuses on process improvement, usually on a single function or single business unit basis—purchasing, planning, or parts and assembly. The effort is internal to the organization and directed at finding the best means of conducting specific supply chain process steps.

An essential tool is *process mapping*. Business processes are carefully analyzed to determine the inputs, outputs, and what happens to convert the inputs to outputs. Flowcharts and other graphics are used to illustrate what is going on. With a full set of process maps illustrating the steps from beginning to end of the supply chain to guide the effort, teams are established to determine where current conditions are not at acceptable standards so that they can improve the processes.

In virtually every instance of supply chain efforts, the beginning emphasis is placed in two major areas: sourcing and logistics. These functions represent the greatest overall business weight—costs—representing anything from 40 to 80 percent of total costs of products sold for a typical manufacturing company. For a service business, logistics may not be as important, but purchasing costs could still be significant.

Beginning with sourcing as the biggest target for weight reduction, the total purchases for a business unit or a company are determined, and the suppliers are identified. There are some easy ways to reduce costs— the number of suppliers is reduced dramatically, product offerings are rationalized, parts are reduced, and the buying volume is leveraged over the smaller supply base for more attractive pricing and features. Substantial gains are typically made in this area, often resulting in a reduction to buying costs of 5 to 8 percent. For example, one $800 million manufacturer of hand tools reduced its supply base from 3,500 to 1,500 companies and, working with the top 100 strategic suppliers, was able to save $35 million in a two-year period.

In the logistics area, the amount of warehousing or distribution center space is analyzed and kept at the level absolutely necessary to hold the goods for actual consumption. Transportation costs are thoroughly reviewed to determine how the cost of outbound freight can be reduced, often cutting the delivery cost per mile by 10 to 20 percent. Many firms spread their shipping contracts over fewer carriers or give up management of trucking fleets to more qualified logistics providers. Internal warehouse and transportation operations are brought to reasonable standards for handling, storing, picking, and delivering the products being stored, while meeting the demands in the market. One major chemical company, for example, analyzed its entire warehousing and distribution system and was able to eliminate half of all space being leased for product storage, while increasing on-time deliveries from 75 to 98 percent.

Many firms get stuck at Level 1. They strongly resist using the full scale of the company or transferring the improvements ideas across the entire company. Content to find savings on a functional or business unit basis, most Level 1 firms are characterized by a silo or stovepipe mentality that prevents the sharing of helpful knowledge. They maintain there is no advantage in centralizing any function or effort or in sharing supply chain improvements. Sourcing savings are not extended to the total purchases of the company, remaining limited to what can be done with individual unit purchases. Information sharing on best practices simply does not exist. Collaboration between functions or business units is resisted, and communication systems that could facilitate processing throughout the organization are nonexistent. The result is an unfortunate case of departmental anarchy, as better practices are not transferred to other business units within the same company.

Level 2—Operational Excellence

In Level 2, the focus changes from the business unit or isolated process. The effort continues on an intraenterprise or internal basis, as the firm begins to recognize the savings being generated and seeks a state of operational excellence in its overall supply chain processing. Most firms are working toward Level 2 in today's business environment.

A focus on ideal conditions begins to spread across the business. The silos and stovepipes separating functions and business units begin to disintegrate, so that the firm can develop best practices across the total organization. This is the level where the Wall Street Diet begins to pay dividends. Three areas yield company-wide dividends—in purchasing, logistics, and forecasting.

Firms expand on the improved capacity developed in Level 1. Now the company's full purchases are leveraged, as category buyers purchase for the total business. For example, one buyer may buy all the furniture needed by a bank or insurance company, ensuring lowest cost is achieved.

Order entry, order processing, and order management become important areas to be improved by the diet. Most firms embark on creating a better and standardized order management system. A communication intranet linking the various parts of the internal business develops so that data on customers and orders can be shared for more reliable processing. The information technology function starts to play an ever-increasing role, providing the technology features needed to enhance any reengineered process steps. As firms analyze their order systems, for example, most find an inordinate number of errors in the processing, an equivalent to consuming too many sweets in the diet. Those firms determined to get lean in this area apply technology to create new order management systems that eliminate mistakes and reduce the need for much of the reconciliation that takes place in cleaning up the mess left by the errors.

Those in purchasing and procurement begin to move to a higher level of buyer-seller relationship where the parties seek supply chain process changes that can benefit both buyer and seller. Taking cues from logistics, the firm realizes that perhaps trucks can be better utilized or warehouse space reduced if the business allies begin sharing data from their planning systems. They can do a better job of matching supply with actual demand without relying on inventory or extra safety stocks. Further savings are found in a sharing atmosphere. Electronic purchasing emerges to handle the lower-value sourcing categories—automating transactions for such items as office supplies, janitorial supplies, and miscellaneous shop materials.

In a typical example, one company found that buying office supplies was taking more than 70 percent of its purchasing personnel time for goods that represented less than 3 percent of total costs. An automated system was introduced to this buying category, cutting the transaction cost and time by almost 80 percent while incidentally eliminating errors with these purchases. This is a dramatic example of how to get lean with a process step.

Logistics embraces the new Wall Street Diet conditions. That function can focus on asset utilization by considering who should own the trucks and employ the drivers. Another focus is the effectiveness of the delivery system—how deliveries should be made and from which holding area. These improvements ensure that the best provider is taking responsibility for the key process steps for accurate and timely delivery, often bypassing the warehouse. Better flow of information through internal automation of transactional activities aids the loaders, shippers, and warehouse personnel to know the actual demand and where any goods might be at any time. This leads directly to satisfying customer needs. Improvements begin to show up in on-time deliveries and fill rates.

Load utilization tends to rise as well, as full truckloads become normal and loads fitting the trucks are found to fill the returning transportation equipment. One consumer products company, working with a major retailer, found both companies had truck fleets that were being used to less than 70 percent of space per truck. By sharing data on actual consumption and replacement needs and available stocks, the companies began using the available space on the trucks, regardless of who owned the equipment. Collaborating to fill up the truck for both inbound and outbound shipments, these firms dramatically reduced the number of trucks needed, while increasing load utilization to over 80 percent.

Demand management becomes an important factor in Level 2 as the firm observes that forecast inaccuracy inhibits accurate planning and manufacturing. With sales forecast accuracy often being as low as 40 percent, the company begins to emphasize the need to get better incoming information on orders and predicted supply needs. Teams are set up to consider the areas of capacity planning and inventory management, with a view toward introducing improved techniques that include better matching of actual customer needs with sensible manufacturing schedules and better order management, without an overload of inventory.

Near the completion of Level 2, some form of sales and operation planning is in effect, with the various functions having an impact on demand management involved in regularly scheduled meetings and interactions to better define the demand signals and matching them with production capacity—in effect blending demand with supply chain planning. Service levels rise, often reaching highs of 95 to 98 percent for key customers. Inventory turns improve, typically from lows of two to three per year, to as high as fifteen to twenty-five or more. At this point, the Wall Street Diet should be working on an internal basis, meaning the house is getting in order to begin external collaboration.

Level 3—Partner Collaboration

Level 1 focuses on key business units; Level 2, on the firm. Level 3 moves beyond the firm to a few carefully selected business allies. This is where the Wall Street Diet becomes difficult for most firms. It's reasonable for our dieter to give up a few desserts or even a drink or two, but at this point the dieter might hit a plateau. In moving from Level 2 to Level 3, the Wall Street Diet asks the firm for more than trimming excess: it must begin changing its lifestyle.

As indicated in Exhibit 3.1, a cultural wall halts further progress by most organizations. This wall warns that external advice is something to be avoided. Most firms find it difficult enough to maintain the gains within the traditional boundaries. This is precisely why the full potential of supply chain management is rarely realized.

To move to Level 3, a firm must break through this wall with a visionary leader. The leader conducts successful pilots that prove the value of participating in the external environment so that others can follow. Once over the wall and into the external environment characterizing Level 3, the firm embarks on interenterprise activities. A powerful new business entity arises—a business network emerges made up of a *few, carefully selected* business allies. Through collaboration with these partners, the Wall Street Diet promotes a higher level of mutual savings. Remember, emphasis is placed on the word *few*. Many firms try to move forward with too many suppliers, distributors, and customers, which invariably bogs down the effort. The successes start with a small number of one-on-one relationships to build a dietary framework for external partnering. This arrangement leads to the formation of value-managed enterprises and the business conditions needed for success.

For example, major defense contractors now rely on a host of network partners, as 80 percent or more of the processing has been outsourced to small, medium, and large subcontractors, in what has become a virtual business-military corporation. This network leverages the capabilities of each member of the supply chain aimed at satisfying the needs of military personnel. Such a network requires each participant or link in the chain to be extremely capable and effective.

Now firms begin to work collaboratively to find the means of distinguishing the network from competing groups or individual companies in the eyes of the target customers. At this level, the strategic sourcing group, for example, invites extremely important suppliers to participate in the sales and operations planning sessions, working on collaborative designs and designing improved business process steps. The hand tool company referenced earlier started working closely with thirty-five key suppliers and ended by collaboratively designing three levels of products—for the home improvement buff, the more serious business contractor, and the heavy industrial user. The result was a shift from Level 2 to Level 3 and a dramatic increase in profitable sales revenues.

In Level 3, the logistics, transportation, and warehousing functions establish relations with qualified supply chain providers, introducing warehouse and transportation management systems. These systems are linked with the better demand signals and key customer needs, and they provide the flow of information that helps all supply chain partners. The whole business network becomes more collaborative, as these functions and others gain access to customer data to drive improved forecasting accuracy, reduce both lead times and delivery cycles, and satisfy key customers. Many firms begin to establish vendor-managed inventory systems with their most important customers and assume responsibility for specific supply functions. Frito-Lay has long been a leader in this area, doing the restocking of shelves and displays for a wide variety of retail customers.

Design and development take a decided leap forward in Level 3, as leading-edge communication tools—based on Internet technology and accomplished through a carefully designed communication extranet—are used to shorten dramatically the time from concept to commercial acceptance. Key partners are directly involved early to codesign and rationalize capabilities, costs, and application of knowledge. For example, automotive companies are moving ahead rapidly with this phase of their supply chain, reducing the time from new car concept to availability in dealer showrooms.

All our research reveals one clear, unambiguous fact: Businesses need to develop operating models to support collaboration within value networks. The dramatic leadership of a few companies demonstrates this approach as the new standard. Without the kind of network in Level 3, companies will wither under increasing costs and defecting customers.

Level 4—Value Chain Constellation

The key differentiator between Level 3 and Level 4 is *advanced* supply chain management. Breaking the cultural wall that separated Level 2 from Level 3 was just the beginning. If Level 3 focuses on sharing information, Level 4 focuses on creating new information, designs, and competitive advantages within the network. Customers are included in more and more decisions and processes across the network. Supplier and customer collaboration blossom in Level 4, as the company moves forward with its positions in one or more networks, or *value chain constellations*. In this advanced external environment, the firm has conducted a clear and defining customer segmentation to target its most desired customer. It begins working in earnest with a small base of suppliers to apply proven features to move into the arena of advanced supply chain management, particularly those involving electronic transfer of business knowledge. It's not unlike members of a dieters' group sharing ideas with each other to get the best overall improvement.

At this level, new tools and metrics appear to gauge the results of the Wall Street Diet. These measures bring attention to the importance of satisfying customers, and on-time deliveries, fill rates, returns, and loss time due to product supply show up on the score card. Network partners begin to use activity-based costing and balanced scorecards to analyze the actual and total costs across the supply chain, with joint teams formed to dig deeper for more improvements. With information being shared electronically, network members start to realize exactly where the opportunities to achieve higher levels of improvement exist, and joint teams are established to find solutions to specific customer problems, involving delays, reshipments, damage, and returns.

Entering this area, a major brewer started working closer with its distributors to find a higher level of savings and found pay dirt. Too much inventory of slower-moving items was languishing in storage because of a lack of shared data on consumption. Working closely with the distributors and using handheld communication devices placed with each truck driver, the company got quicker access to actual consumption data, while providing the distributors with better access to manufacturing and delivery schedules. The end result was an increase in sales through fresher products delivered on time and the reduction of inventories by almost 20 percent.

On the supply side, supplier relationship management becomes a feature of advanced efforts. Working together, buyers and sellers focus on the categories of most importance in the purchase and look at the total cost of ownership, to define the areas where both partners can contribute to the next level of improvement. A similar tact is taken on the customer side, as customer relationship management develops as a network feature, involving serious data sharing and developing joint strategies and business goals aimed at increasing revenues for both parties, through better analysis of trends and customer needs. (More information will be supplied on this facet of supply chain in Chapter 8.)

Level 4 progress depends on the application of e-commerce and e-business communication techniques to enable end-to-end transparency in what is occurring across the value chain network. That means the linked businesses share data on what is in demand, what is anywhere in the end-to-end processing, and any constraints that could inhibit flow to the consumer.

Two special features appear in this level: collaborative design and manufacturing, and collaborative planning, forecasting, and replenishment. In the first case, selective supplier assistance is used to greatly reduce cycle time for new and innovative product and service development and to improve the likelihood of market success. Managing the product or service over its full life cycle becomes a joint effort. Aerospace, automotive, and defense groups are well along in these areas. The drive in automotive, for example, is to deliver a car to a consumer in less than ten days after selection. In the second case, after a slow start, suppliers and large retailers are now working together to share actual data on customer demand, through cash register sales and available supply, to improve forecast accuracy and drive down replenishment costs. Wal-Mart and Kroger have made particularly good strides in this area.

Level 5—Full Network Connectivity

Level 5 is more theoretical than actual at this time. Level 5 requires new levels of trust, transparency, and involvement. There are no vestiges of adversarial relations. What had been characterized as a network emerges to look more like a new enterprise. This level is characterized by what we call full network connectivity, the ultimate result of the Wall Street Diet. Finely tuned business systems are shared across the value-managed enterprise. This is the world of full network collaboration and the use of technology to gain positions of market dominance. The companies forming the value network break down resistance to sharing knowledge and establish the communications links necessary to transfer vital information on supplies, inventories, goods in transit, warehouse stocks, and so forth, to enable better network responses with the lowest total cost. Once again, picture a group of dieters being photographed for the after conditions, following their dramatic and collective improvements.

It is in Level 5 that a shoe firm, for example, can look across its total business enterprise and see with extremely high accuracy exactly how much raw material is coming together for the fabrication of the first part of the eventual pair of running shoes that will be delivered to the Foot Locker retail outlet in the Houston Galleria shopping center. In-transit shipments can be accessed and diversions made to stores more in need of a particular shoe or size. The vision is at the very precise level of the needed shoe, for excess inventories no longer exist. Speed to market is achieved since there is no downtime left to absorb profits. Similarly, an insurance company can view claims processing online in real time, or a car dealership can access inventories to find a particular model with features needed by a specific customer.

Only a few organizations per industry have reached this level, but those that do introduce unprecedented accuracy and cycle times across the end-to-end networks that are now totally electronically enabled. In later chapters, we will describe the interenterprise collaboration and technology systems needed to make this part of the Wall Street Diet work successfully.

The enterprise at Level 5 has come a long way from the parochial business unit perspective at the beginning of the first level. Every business unit not only has transformed but has done so in the context of every other unit up to and including satisfying the customer.

CALIBRATING SUCCESS WITH THE DIET

Through research and firsthand experiences, we have developed a chart that measures progress with the Wall Street Diet (see Exhibit 3.2). Important areas affected by the diet are noted on the horizontal axis, and the vertical axis measures points of new profit that can be added as a percentage of revenue. We suggest that any firm pursuing the diet should prepare and maintain a similar chart showing the actual improvement for the categories displayed and other factors of importance to the business. Most firms will find savings in each of these areas; they are the minimum.

EXHIBIT 3.2 The Wall Street Diet Success Chart

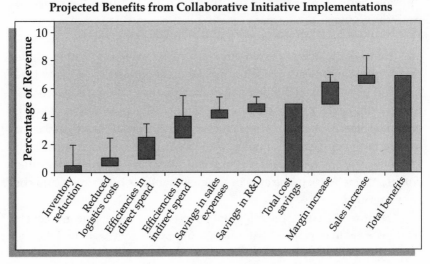

Projected Benefits from Collaborative Initiative Implementations

Exhibit 3.2 reflects actual result ranges for a large number of firms. The projected benefits are depicted in ranges because each firm will have greater or lesser success depending on the importance of the category, the baseline, and the effort given to that part of the diet.

The chart begins with inventory, which we know can add up to two points of new profit to a firm through lower storage and carrying costs and a lesser need for working capital. We portray a two-point potential range and fill in only about one-third of a profit point. Most companies do not reap the full benefit, as they simply force the inventories onto obliging upstream suppliers who hold the goods until needed. Such a move appears as an improvement to the firm's working capital and inventory carrying charges. If a supplier simply adds such costs into its pricing, there has been no real network savings—the fat has just been moved around. The better technique is to introduce visibility across the network, pursue a network diet that eliminates the need for the inventory, and be responsive enough to have the needed goods in the right amount ready at the time and point of need.

Similar steps are taken for reducing logistics costs, for savings sales expense, and for decreasing research and development costs. These improvements from the lean diet should result in about five points of new profits from emphasis on the cost side of the financial statement.

We advise that any firm using the Wall Street Diet should construct a similar chart, but with the appropriate categories and realistic ranges of improvement. Actual results can then be used to fill in the ranges as progress is made.

The chart does not begin and end with cost savings. As the disciplines and results of the diet are taken into the areas of marketing and sales, further improvements are possible. As the chart indicates, another three points of improvement are possible as the firm uses the benefits of the diet to increase margins and build new revenues. This potential will be discussed in later chapters as we explain how the Wall Street Diet forges the path toward use of customer intelligence and the creation of a value-managed network focused on customer service and satisfaction, which truly differentiates the network in the eyes of the most important customers and consumer groups.

The firm will realize the full profit potential as it moves toward Level 5. It is important to remember that dramatic improvements begin with Level 3.

Up until then, marginal gains are earned, to be sure, but the focus of the diet is greatly improved health and well-being for the long term. The loss of a few pounds can make the dieter feel better, and clothes will fit better, but beware of backsliding. Changed lifestyles begin only with Level 3.

A FUTURE FOCUS GUIDES THE DIET

When a firm and its closest business partners approach the highest and most appropriate level of the supply chain maturity model, they begin in earnest to use the Wall Street Diet for achieving a level of success that typically eludes most businesses. With an agreement to pursue the diet together and with focused goals that will lead to industry dominance, the players now pursue building network business together. New and extremely powerful new tools support the network.

Joint sourcing finds lowest delivered and total cost for all constituents.

Working within a virtual logistics environment, where the trucks are filled by finding open space through computer analysis, is included as a new tool.

Joint sales calls on targeted customers can complete the loop and lead to new and profitable revenues.

Comanaging inventory to meet actual demand is another tool, as well as adapting product design to take advantage of new materials and breakthrough engineering.

Integrated business solutions that better meet the servicing needs of customers are codeveloped, as the partners analyze the vast amounts of knowledge stored in their collective databases and develop responses that are tuned to what the data say the market is demanding.

The effort continues with the firms working together to develop the value-managed enterprise with the overall objective of business development for all key members of the network.

CONTEMPORARY BUSINESS MODEL

How does the Wall Street Diet work in practice? We will describe many examples as we pursue the diet's elements and the inherent new practices it demands. Before a firm can emerge into higher levels, it must streamline processes across the firm. For example, a firm must rationalize its product line before moving to higher levels. The lessons learned in that effort will accrue to the enterprise throughout the network.

For now, consider what is happening with the biggest packaged-foods manufacturer in the United States. Kraft Foods Inc. had bulked up over the years with many acquisitions and new product introductions. During a time when scale of operation was a measure of success, Kraft rode high on the charts. With the pressure now on meeting consumer demand better than any competitor and rapid turnover of goods at the retail level, the bulk may be too great. We mean the firm was not lean in terms of having only the right products and inventory necessary to meet current demand, was not providing the shortest possible cycle times, or had extra lead times to ensure delivery.

Under the direction of new CEO Roger Deromedi, the firm is determined to slim down. Deromedi put Kraft on the diet by selling the Life Savers and Altoids brands to Wrigley. He began ridding Kraft of products not central to its overall objectives. Other divestures are planned as "laggard and peripheral" product lines are removed from the corporate portfolio, so the company can concentrate on those brands commanding a dominant market position—a means of ensuring lean operations in what is kept. And, true to our diet objective, customer satisfaction helps in the decision making. According to the new CEO, "We want the products that consumers and retailers are more excited about" (Arndt 2004: 46).

Like other consumer products manufacturers, the pressure is on to meet the increasing demands from the retail giants such as Wal-Mart, which have little patience for excesses in their supply chains. With these retailers only interested in those products that arrive in time to meet demand, without incurring stock-outs and with products on the shelf that move swiftly to consumers, there is no room for fat or poor responsiveness: You cannot have clogged arteries. Too many variations of the same old and tired products that block the flow do not fit the new mold. Reduction of Stock Keeping Units (SKUs) by Procter & Gamble and Unilever have set the course in this area, as the new focus is on matching demand with supply of the right products, so manufacturer and retailer both achieve high levels of turnover at the store level. The flow is quicker, more responsive to needs, and not encumbered with extra costs.

SUMMARY

We began this chapter referring to the importance of the cardiovascular system and the life-threatening blockages. Businesses have a similar system—the supply chain.

The supply chain maturity model is an excellent way to focus attention on how much progress has been made with such an effort and specifically where the business is still bogged down—order entry, planning, scheduling, inventory management, warehousing, on-time delivery, billing, and so forth.

- At Level 1, the dieting firm loses waste and costs in individual business units.
- At Level 2, the dieting firm sheds waste and costs across the entire company.
- At Level 3, the dieting firm trims waste and costs in an evolving network with a few key strategic allies. Lifestyle is changing.
- At Level 4, the firm has switched from losing waste and costs into developing new tone and strength across the network with the help of a few trusted business partners.
- At Level 5, the firm is part of a strong, profitable network at the peak of financial health and well-being.

A business needs to evaluate the performance of its supply chain to determine where a health-threatening obstacle might exist. The technique of analyzing progress and calibrating where a business unit might be on the chart and determining the gap between current and potential performance is equivalent to following a plan to change lifestyle to avoid a cholesterol/circulation problem.

Eating better is similar to getting the right resources to the right areas at the right time with the ultimate goal of satisfying the customer who is part of the process.

In some life-threatening situations, the equivalent to medication or surgery is to bring in outside expertise to help determine what better practices can be substituted for what has been identified as a weak link in the processing.

Supply chain management is alive and well as a business improvement activity. It is also maturing as firms have been pursuing improvements for nearly twenty years. By reducing the clogging, lowering the supply chain cholesterol, and solving business health problems, the Wall Street Diet helps your company find advanced supply chain conditions that differentiate the firm and its network partners from the competition.

CHECKLIST FOR SENIOR MANAGEMENT

☐ Select a business unit or business function to test the diet. Provide every conceivable kind of support to attain the vision.

☐ Identify a leader or champion who will embrace the diet. Together, determine a range of potential impact on the business unit's performance and enhancement to the firm's financial statement. Allow the leader to set the parameters for the diet—resources needed, timeframe for accomplishment, action steps, and potential alliances to be pursued.

☐ Be that leader's champion and facilitator.

☐ Give the leader responsibility and authority, and prevent the naysayers from derailing the effort.

☐ Smooth the way among other business units and companies in the evolving network.

☐ Start now.

CHECKLIST FOR FUNCTIONAL MANAGERS AND DIET CHAMPIONS

☐ With the help of a single key supplier, manufacturer, and distributor, draw a process or value stream map of what happens across the linked supply chain—the extended enterprise.

☐ Mutually identify, just as a doctor would with an X-ray or similar tool, the areas with problems—bottlenecks, constraints, poor delivery times, cycle times lower than the industry average, long lead times, and so forth.

☐ Use a partnering diagnostic lab (explained in the appendix) to help identify five or six key steps to improve the conditions.

- ☐ Establish an action plan to eliminate these problems with a timetable and required resources. Make a reasonable estimate of the costs and benefits that will be derived from this effort. Then get busy getting rid of the problems.
- ☐ Identify bottlenecks or wasted activities at your location or within your function.
- ☐ Do not acquire safety stock to make up for poor forecasting.
- ☐ Understand and work with key strategic suppliers.
- ☐ Start now.

Lose Weight—
Make Your Business Lean

Most dieters have a common focus—lose weight. We will stress throughout this book that it is important to consider more than weight loss; lifestyle and exercise are also critical elements.

Even so, the common measure of success is simply, "How much weight have you lost?" Without doubt, losing weight is vitally important. Being overweight threatens your health and mobility; more serious obesity can kill. We will talk about measure and diagnosis in determining success, but in this chapter, we also want to address weight loss directly.

For business, too, this chapter is about shedding excess pounds—from inventory, bad policies and procedures, errors and mistakes, weak supply chain processes, inhibiting cultural views, and waste in general. Waste in a business is relatively easy to identify. Just ask, "Does this activity add value?" Inventory adds no value until you use it to make something or the finished product is purchased. Those garments on a rack in a retail store have no value until a customer makes a purchase.

Across an enterprise, lean activities do add value, which is why lean is a central ingredient in the Wall Street Diet. A successful dieter knows weight loss is not a one-time activity. Nor is the elimination of waste.

Every diet has a starting point: a desire to seek meaningful change and improvement. The recommended first step should be a checkup using the Wall Street Diet calibration tool. And as you calibrate, remember that a successful diet is part of a lifestyle change; for a company, that means adopting a new business model.

This chapter will provide background on the notion of lean and introduce ways to apply that concept across the enterprise, from raw materials to final consumption. Our version of lean is based on the concepts of lean manufacturing as epitomized by Toyota, where the whole idea is to reduce or eliminate *muda* (the Japanese term for *waste*). The lean enterprise extends the concept of reducing waste to all of your customers and suppliers. Simply put, you only sell what your customers want, when and where they want it. You only receive the right goods, services, and materials from your suppliers when you need them. Lean is about eliminating waste in any business, in any segment, in any activity. Lean in a bank would be eliminating multiple customer information systems, being able to know everything about bank customers and all their transactions in one place. Lean in a retail outlet would minimize customer returns, without alienating consumers with incomprehensible return policies.

Lean is a technique that can be applied to any business function or process.

The Wall Street Diet uses advanced supply chain management as the tool to reduce a firm's cholesterol, lower blood pressure to healthy levels, and increase cardiovascular flow. When we consider the lean enterprise, we will consider the Business Body Mass Indicator (BBMI). The human BMI is a measurement of body fat based on height and weight. BBMI similarly is a measurement of size (revenue) and weight (profit). Fat—in this case, business waste—reduces profits because it consists of unneeded product, inventory, process steps, and so forth. In the interconnected business world, fat anywhere in the supply chain eventually decreases profits across the enterprise.

The manufacturing BBMI analysis tool is more complicated than entering your height and weight. You will work to analyze your company's operating conditions, but the payoff is improved performance. For the manufacturing company, the business diet tool shown in Exhibit 4.1 is designed to be used with key trading partners in the enterprise. A quick glance will show that lean manufacturing is not the end state but rather an interim goal leading to the ideal manufacturing state—adaptability to current market conditions.

Manufacturing leaders are moving aggressively beyond lean to flexible and adaptive solutions that fit their strategic goal. Lean manufacturing can be the end state of a manufacturing strategy based on capacity utilization. Flexible and adaptive characteristics bring ultimate utilization of

EXHIBIT 4.1 Business Body Mass Index (BBMI)

Action Points →

Progression — Business Functions	Level 1/2 Mass Production	Level 3 Lean Manufacturing	Level 4 Flexible Manufacturing	Level 5 Adaptive Manufacturing
Business Goal	Standardization Cost Reduction	Reduce Waste	Optimize Responsiveness	Standardization Cost Reduction
Design, Development Product/Service Introduction	Internal only	Selected external assistance	Collaborative design—enterprise integration and PIM linked CAD/CIM	Business functional view—joint design and development
Purchasing, Procurement, Sourcing	Leverage business unit volume	Leverage fuel network through aggregation	Key supplier assistance, web-based sourcing	Network sourcing through best constituent
Marketing, Sales, Customer Service	Internally developed programs, promotions	Customer-focused, data-based initiatives	Collaborative development for focused consumer base	Consumer response system across the value chain
Planning, Scheduling, Manufacturing	MRP MRPII DRP	ERP—Kanban, lean processes	Collaborative network planning (S&CP)—lean enterprise	Full network business system optimization, shared processes and systems
Logistics	Manufacturing push—inventory incentive	Pull system through internal/external providers	Best constituent provider—dual channel	Total network, dual-channel optimization
Customer Care	Customer service reaction	Focused service—call centers	Segmented response system, customer relationship mgt.	Matched care—customer care automation and remediation
Continuous Improvement	TQM	QFD/Six Sigma	Interenterprise Six Sigma	Enterprise quality management, single point of accountability
Information Technology	Point solutions Internal silos	Linked intranets Corp. strategy/architecture	Internet-based extranet shared capabilities	Full network communication system shared architecture planning

capacity and design, tooling and manufacturing processes, and market responsiveness. The majority of businesses will be concentrating on moving from Level 1 and 2 to more advanced levels. If you wonder, "Can we skip levels?" the answer is no, but some parts of the firm may have footprints in various levels simultaneously. Companies that try to skip levels will be unable to absorb all of the necessary changes.

ACHIEVING LEAN CONDITIONS

The starting point is a focus on getting the body to lean conditions. Lean techniques are enjoying a renaissance. At one time, companies declared victory by reducing the number of gondolas or work positions in a work cell. Today, companies have come to realize that just shuffling inventory around and optimizing the use of a few square feet of factory space for a time does not bring long-term benefit to the bottom line or enhance share price.

Other companies are trying to catch the leaders by using lean without understanding where they are going. This effort underscores the difficulty and often the fallacy of benchmarking. Companies traditionally benchmark one isolated element or process—quality, scheduling, plant operations, or store layout. They fail to realize that you have to make substantive changes in related or adjoining areas for substantive improvements. Isolation leads to short-sighted goals. These companies will never catch—or become—the leaders this way.

Exhibit 4.1 gives you a desired end state as your target, with steps along the way as guidelines. It can be customized for a particular firm in a particular industry. Now consider some pertinent questions: Do you begin your regimen with supply chain efforts? Where do you apply lean techniques? How do you add the quality ingredient? The answers depend on where you are in the beginning. The exhibit shows progress by business function and can be applied as a worksheet to help guide a firm from its current position sequentially to the more desired position. Exhibit 4.2 is a blank worksheet to help grade your current position and map out the most appropriate next steps. An interactive BBMI and a more in-depth guide are available for this purpose at www.thewallstreetdiet.com.

Using the worksheet, compare your company's or business unit's position by row with the best practices shown in Exhibit 4.1. Add a check mark to the cell you think your company and its business partners occupy. Each check in the first level is worth zero points, each check in the

EXHIBIT 4.2 Business BMI Chart

	Level 1/2	Level 3	Level 4	Level 5	Functional BMI
Design, Development Product/Service Introduction					
Purchasing, Procurement, Sourcing					
Marketing, Sales, Customer Service					
Planning, Scheduling, Manufacturing					
Logistics					
Customer Care					
Continuous Improvement					
Information Technology					

Composite BBMI

second level is worth two points, each check in the third level is worth five points, and, finally, each check in the fourth level is worth ten points. Take a look at your composite BBMI score and then your functional BBMI scores by row. If your total BBMI is between 0 and 15, you are operating as a mass production company. Look at the rows for low scores—0s, for example. Use those scores as a guide to which specific areas you can improve, raising your functional BBMI. That way, your activities become focused and achievable.

A perfect BBMI is 80. An honest appraisal generally reveals no single company achieves eighty points, but an exceptional business could score 50 to 55. We use a tool with a nearly unreachable goal because leading firms have these objectives as targets, and we want you to build a company that is as healthy in fifty years as it is in five.

The exercise is not trivial, and the interactive guide at www.thewall streetdiet.com might better suit your purposes. While many tools are available to help you understand lean capabilities, they will not give you an overall business BMI and may leave out important diagnostic information. You would not trust a diagnosis if a physician put you on a regimen for losing weight by merely taking your pulse.

The beginning of the exercise uses the time-honored method pioneered by Toyota, *genbutsu*, which is literally translated as "the real thing" or "actual material." A looser translation is "go and see." The application of genbutsu to lean processing was made mandatory by Toyota in its approach to lean.

Imagine you are touring one of your plants. You look about and see inventory, or you know inventory is on the way. You look at the facilities, machinery, and a handful of workers. You may even develop a value stream map. What do you see, and what have you missed? Perhaps you can say, "We don't have any excess inventory." Now ask, "Is there excess inventory at our supplier's location? In transit? In a warehouse?" If any answer is yes, you add to this model a view of the extended enterprise, taking into account the entire inventory. Look at raw materials, transportation, storage and warehousing, cost of capital, and so forth. Then seek out the waste you should be eliminating. The essence of the lean enterprise is the annihilation of waste, whether it is on your books or those of a business partner. You are still paying for it.

As you "go and see," what are you looking for? Watch for repeated trips, backtracking, multiple lift-truck runs, expedited shipping, demurrage charges, rework, and other non-value-adding activities. Look at how your uncoordinated changes create the "bullwhip effect" (overreacting on the upstream side to downstream changes in a supply chain demand) on your suppliers and lead to overstock conditions before your customers. Use "go and see" to find the typical invisible inventory and processes of your customers and suppliers. Discover how they do things that you think could positively affect your company, such as their administrative processes.

This exercise should not be done alone. You must work with your customers and suppliers to accomplish a solid view of conditions. The approach advised by the Wall Street Diet would have you extend such mapping to the entire value stream, as you bring all constituents in to map and evaluate improvement opportunities jointly. The beauty of the federated keiretsu described in Chapter 2 is that you can develop this model quickly, without the financial investment and colocation of the traditional keiretsu.

Exhibit 4.3 shows that the lean enterprise must have a simultaneous top-down and bottom-up view. Add to that perspective the horizontal components of your extended supply chain. Exhibit 4.4 shows how the extended team is designed for total enterprise optimization. The future business state is a lean enterprise with greater network capabilities from the view of the most important customers. It will optimize a value chain as never before. From a business perspective aimed at such a condition, the Wall Street Diet and its inherent ingredients are applied as the route to a slim body (the extended enterprise) and a routine that maintains the desired performance (optimized costs) so that greater revenues are generated through greater customer satisfaction.

We have discussed the second ingredient of the Wall Street Diet, the renewed emphasis on lean, using the Toyota production system as an example. The methodology began as a means of allowing the Japanese firm to compete against much stronger and established firms. It is now a concept that has been adopted and modified by hundreds of companies in a host of industries across virtually all business functions. The new approach has an entry price, however. It must empower the people who will carry out the improved processes, so that they truly believe they are adding value. They must not fall back into weak practices, which will surely cause them to regain their former weight at a later time. Exhibit 4.3 shows the level of involvement necessary, while Exhibit 4.4 shows an organization structure designed to build your lean enterprise.

EXHIBIT 4.3   Lean Enterprise Approach

Establishing Effective, Tightly Linked Performance Measures

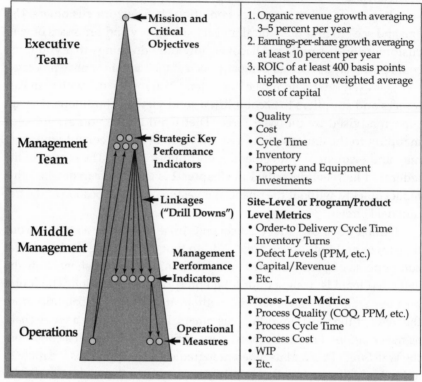

Executive Team	← Mission and Critical Objectives	1. Organic revenue growth averaging 3–5 percent per year 2. Earnings-per-share growth averaging at least 10 percent per year 3. ROIC of at least 400 basis points higher than our weighted average cost of capital
Management Team	← Strategic Key Performance Indicators	• Quality • Cost • Cycle Time • Inventory • Property and Equipment Investments
Middle Management	← Linkages ("Drill Downs") Management Performance ← Indicators	**Site-Level or Program/Product Level Metrics** • Order-to Delivery Cycle Time • Inventory Turns • Defect Levels (PPM, etc.) • Capital/Revenue • Etc.
Operations	Operational ← Measures	**Process-Level Metrics** • Process Quality (COQ, PPM, etc.) • Process Cycle Time • Process Cost • WIP • Etc.

COQ - Cost of quality
PPM - Parts per million

Quality and lean are mutually fulfilling ingredients in the diet. Quality and quality standards are amplified in other chapters, but we want to note here that the two ingredients are inexorably linked. Exhibit 4.5 compares lean and Six Sigma. If you look at the high-level comparisons, you can see how these processes fit together very well. However, lean and quality are not enough, as they are often confined within the four walls of a single company. The Wall Street Diet also indicates a distinct need for joint governance, including quality processes.

What is the practical model to use? The Wall Street Diet recommends the approach shown in Exhibit 4.6. Again, the key to success is collaboration. The model shows that there must be a strategic mechanism, the joint

EXHIBIT 4.4   Lean Enterprise Governance

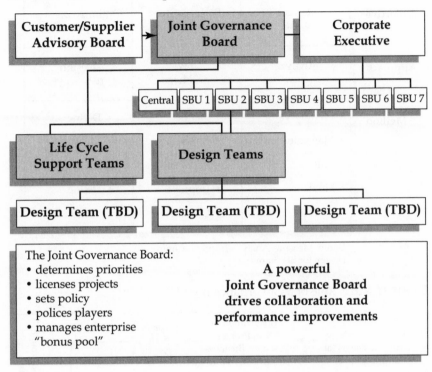

The Joint Governance Board:
- determines priorities
- licenses projects
- sets policy
- polices players
- manages enterprise "bonus pool"

**A powerful
Joint Governance Board
drives collaboration and
performance improvements**

governance board, and a tactical level in place. Why the tactical level? First, genbutsu demands it. "Go and see" is the key mechanism for success in these endeavors, with the people actually doing the work as a critical element, because they have a lot of value to add through their in-depth knowledge of the situation.

A dashboard is another key element of measurement. Metrics are extremely important in our extended enterprise, more than ever before. When you implement the model being described or are asked by one of your business partners to participate, you can expect skepticism. Solid results are the only way to overcome that normal uncertainty. The dashboard captures the improving metrics and shares them with all key participants. Dashboard metrics are up to you to define, but some key ones are inventory turns, work in progress, project status, stock levels, and so forth.

EXHIBIT 4.5 Process Comparisons—Lean and Six Sigma

	Lean	Six Sigma DMAIC*	DFSS†
Objective	Reduce waste	Reduce errors (existing processes)	Optimize process (new processes)
Approach	Analyze flow	Fix problems	Design new ways
Method	• Identify value • Map value stream • Pull • Flow • Perfect	• Define • Measure • Analyze • Improve • Control	• Define • Measure • Analyze • Define • Verify

*Define-Measure-Analyze-Improve-Control
†Design for Six Sigma

EXHIBIT 4.6 Role of a Governance Board

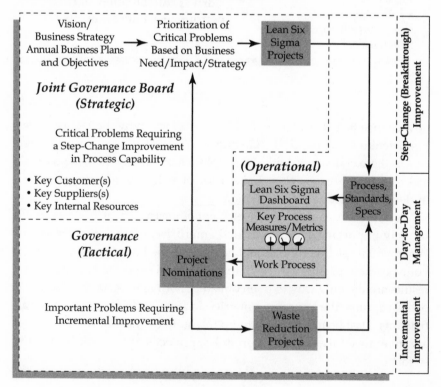

Important projects originate at the governance board level. That way executives are prepared to support these projects and explain the expected benefits to all of the constituents. Before trying to execute the recommended approach broadly, start with a key customer and supplier. Do not choose the project first; choose the partners. If the effort is truly collaborative, the decision should be made in concert.

This approach has multiple benefits. First, you are walking the talk—beginning with collaboration, not ending with it. Second, you will also uncover the objections, roadblocks, and cultural inhibitors before you start. Third, with everyone having a stake in the game, you have a higher probability of success. The project should also be small, of short duration, and easily measured.

LEAN ENTERPRISE BACKGROUND

The benefits of lean manufacturing have been well documented, and the fundamentals can be found in two books by Shingo (1982, 1985). Attention outside Japan was particularly established in the seminal book on the subject, *The Machine That Changed the World* (Womack, Jones, and Roos 1990), which was written by a group from the International Motor Vehicle Program (IMVP), an effort started in 1985 at the Massachusetts Institute of Technology (MIT). The intention of IMVP was "to explore creative mechanisms for industry-government-university interaction on an international basis in order to understand the fundamental forces of industrial change and improve the policy-making process in dealing with change" (Womack et al. 1990: 4).

Two key figures emerge from this book. Eiji Toyoda (a son of the company founder) and Taiichi Ohno (head of manufacturing) decided to take the Toyota Motor Company into serious competition with the two leading U.S. manufacturers. Ohno developed the Toyota manufacturing system as the only means he could see to go up against the American competitors. The company eventually honed the system that vaulted the firm to the head of the class in the automotive industry.

Working from a simple formula, Ohno determined that the giants in a near-monopolistic environment set the market price as being equal to the costs plus the desired profit margin. These giants were able to stake out the costs, which they determined using finely tuned industrial engineering techniques. Stated simply, the formula was

$$Price = Cost + Profit$$

In effect, the giant companies could control all three factors.

Under the conditions he was facing, Ohno had no choice but to change the formula to reflect the profit margin he determined was needed for survival and prosperity. He decided that margin was then equal to the market price, over which he had little control at the time, less his costs. The revised formula became

$$Profit = Market\ Price - Costs$$

With an understanding that he could control only one factor—costs—Ohno began to develop what became termed *lean production* by IMVP researcher John Krafcik. Under Ohno's direction, the firm set out to eliminate all waste—time, effort, materials, quality, costs, and so forth. Toyota realized quickly its workers would be a key to success. The workers orchestrated the desired elimination of waste, at one point delivering forty implemented ideas per employee per year.

Two primary criteria of measurement were used in the early years—yield and quality—to achieve high production rates with as few quality problems as possible. This proved to be a very solid strategy. A remarkable insight by Ohno was to insist that the new system would entail virtually no rework—a major factor in waste. That meant the identification of a defective part was the key to improvement, and the root cause was to be eliminated so that it did not cause later problems in the assembly process. Workers were empowered to stop any assembly line when defects were noted, and teams would flock to the area of concern and work on a solution until the problem was corrected—forever.

Total enterprise optimization will never be achieved without elimination of wastes and redundancies.

UNDERSTANDING THE LEAN ENTERPRISE

For the purposes of the Wall Street Diet, the lean concepts mean the firm and its business allies must work together to remove all non-value-adding activities—that is, clear the arteries to build a strong and responsive body.

By adding the modern features possible through electronic communication, current systems include visual routings and visual *kanbans*—the areas allotted for the placement of parts or supplies prior to actual use in assembly or processing.

Statistical analysis is applied to determine root causes of problems—control charts, histograms, Pareto charts, and trend charts.

Quality is built into the processing at each step, and intelligence integrated across the enterprise becomes the differentiating factor, as all parts of the business gain access to the knowledge needed to eliminate all waste.

Unified transactions and summaries are straightforward and available to those who need the data. Performance is monitored in a real-time environment, and questions are answered as swiftly and accurately as possible with the available technology. In essence, a lean enterprise is a business network that reduces all waste and optimizes the use of all resources, not just on a factory floor or in a hospital, but everywhere in the extended supply chain. That means lean is applied from product development or concept of supply to delivery of products and services with the help of all supporting activities, especially information technology.

The lean enterprise, moreover, will align the efforts of key constituents through strong collaboration and sharing of vital knowledge. Relations with suppliers are enhanced to become a source of competitive advantage. Essentially, the lean enterprise embraces a systematic approach to identifying and eliminating waste through continuous improvement by matching the supply with the demand under near-perfect conditions. That means the customer gets exactly what is wanted when it is needed, and only what is needed.

Under the lean microscope, non-value-adding activities, including transporting material and supplies, inspecting finished goods, and checking and storing inventory, are candidates for elimination. One of the most important tenets is that there must be an accepted baseline from which improvement would be measured. In a modern sense, the mission of a lean enterprise is to deliver the greatest customer satisfaction and improve the chances of success. When implemented, the benefits will include the elimination of non-value-added work, no errors, and zero failures, defects, and returns. It will also include greater utilization of all resources—people, machines, and time—and meticulous maintenance of machinery and equipment with perfect safety records.

In layman's terms, lean has three components:

- A toolbox of techniques and methods for improving any part of the operating model
- A philosophy that emphasizes elimination of all waste and optimization of all resources
- A system through which a company and its closest business allies can deliver continuous improvement

LEAN'S IMPACT ON MANUFACTURING

Lean techniques eliminate non-value-adding activities. That means those participating in the Wall Street Diet must adopt a pull approach to their system, in which a "pacemaker" or critical process step sets the rhythm of production.

Developing the rhythm requires a clear understanding of the actual demand driving the processing. Weak sales forecasts can no longer be at the center of planning and response. Rather, the emphasis is on determining the actual demand and matching it as squarely as possible with the supply and flow of products and services.

Forecasts coming from disparate sources—sales, manufacturing, marketing, customers, point-of-sale—in various units or monies, from various geographies, must be translated into highly accurate formats. The end result must become a demand signal that is within less than 1 percent of full accuracy for supply and manufacturing requirements. Managing by exception, because of the inevitable market aberrations encountered, is a feasible feature, but it must be based on user-defined exception of an extremely small magnitude, with proactive efforts to eliminate such future aberrations. (Forecasts and forecast accuracy are discussed in greater detail in Chapter 6.)

In a manufacturing environment, lean focuses on single-unit production and inventory accuracy for that single unit with no more and no less. Based on specific demand, kanbans are used to manage the pull of materials and components into production and assembly, with just-in-time delivery without extra safety stocks. Lean manufacturing results under these conditions in less—less space, less time for completion, less inventory, less cost, and less rework and returns.

APPLYING LEAN TECHNIQUES
TO SUPPLY CHAINS

From a supply chain perspective, the lean concepts are extended to incorporate new boundaries of the extended enterprise, including the key business partners and processes. Again, the idea is that all excess inventory and redundant processes are a waste that drives up costs and makes operations more complex. Implementation of standards developed and accepted by the key partners will be used to monitor and control the processes. Most important, the benefits derived from the greater capabilities will result in mutual rewards for all constituents contributing to the lean implementation.

To establish a definition, we call the *lean supply chain* a collaborating set of businesses linked by the end-to-end flows of products and service, information and knowledge, and finances, resulting in total enterprise optimization gained through total elimination of waste and increased revenues gained through greater customer satisfaction.

Looking at Exhibit 4.3 again, we see that the concept combines a top-to-bottom as well as a bottom-to-top approach to bring lean concepts and applications to a lean supply chain. Four levels of tightly linked performance must be achieved. Beginning at the base level of operations, operational metrics must be at industry-best, including process quality (cost of quality, good parts per million), process cycle times, process costs, and inventory levels. These measures, moreover, must be linked directly to the strategic key performance indicators established by the collective management teams.

In the middle management layer, the performance indicators revolve around site-level or program- and product-level metrics, which include order-to-delivery time, inventory turns, defect levels, use of capital, and revenue increases. Again, there should be a direct link with the performance indicators established by the network partners for these key measures. The management team will establish those measures, focusing top-level attention on quality, cost, cycle time, inventory, and property and equipment investments involving network assets. The final linkage is to where it all starts, with the executive team decision made to differentiate the network in the eyes of the key customers or consumer groups. Here the driving mission-critical objectives are established. Examples are given to cover a revenue growth target, a goal for earnings per share (a popular total supply chain target), and return on invested capital (ROIC).

Contemporary supply chains feature lean techniques as a key ingredient for waste elimination and process improvement.

CONTEMPORARY BUSINESS MODELS

Whirlpool Corporation offers an example of a firm using lean techniques to gain a business advantage. Back in 2001, the supply chain organization of this major appliance manufacturer was part of Whirlpool's business that the salespeople often mocked as their "sales disablers." Availability of product, for example, hovered around 87 percent. In a move to correct this condition, the firm decided to achieve world-class capabilities in supply chain performance by focusing foremost on customer requirements.

In an approach that worked from consumer needs back to operations, the immediate focus was on what the company identified as "delivery with integrity," a measure having high significance for the buyers of appliances. "Give a date, hit a date," was the driving motto. Working with key customers—Sears, Lowes, and Best Buy—the firm identified requirements by market segment and the "27 different dimensions along which performance was being judged" (Slone 2004: 117). The team charged with making the necessary improvements then benchmarked expectations and current results against industry-best performance. With a fix on what would be industry-best performance, the team went forward to find what could be accomplished at low levels of investment.

An early success came about with the introduction of a new sales and operations planning (S&OP) process. This effort advanced into a collaborative planning forecasting and replenishment (CPFR) pilot. Within thirty days of launch, forecast error was cut in half, a significant advance since the firm reckons "a one-point improvement in forecast accuracy reduces total finished goods by several million dollars." Within a year, Whirlpool had historic low inventories with a high service level. Finished goods working capital was reduced by 10 percent, and total cost productivity improved by 5.1 percent. By May 2002, an Internet survey showed the company rated as "most improved" and "most progressive" (Slone 2004: 119).

We have stated that lean has an impact beyond manufacturing. The best opportunities for applying lean are within processes that span the supply chain network. The following example demonstrates two key Wall Street Diet precepts: lean supply chain and collaboration.

Cost and performance issues impact all organizations. A lean supply chain can offer two seemingly contradictory benefits: decreased inventory costs and increased product availability. An example is presented through a collaborative project between a large aerospace and defense contractor and Computer Sciences Corporation (CSC). A European air force needed to improve aircraft availability—the key customer requirement—and decrease inventory costs for its depots supporting a fighter aircraft program. The military is in a particularly difficult position, as it must have high aircraft availability while remaining cost-conscious in these days of skyrocketing prices. These two goals are often seen as contradictory. The emphasis is always on aircraft availability, and that is the message most widely communicated. When all the constituents were involved and they had tools to use and could suggest how to reduce operational costs as well as improve availability, everyone could focus on both success factors.

The approach used lean techniques to modify current processes. In particular, Genbutsu and spaghetti diagrams with Six Sigma tools were used to analyze the processes for improvement. A rigorously designed training program allowed everyone involved in the process to understand the new lean warehousing approach. The team engaged all the constituents in this project and sought improvement ideas from anyone involved: air crews, warehouse personnel, trainers, purchasing staff, and management.

The solution was developed collaboratively, led by the contractor, with integrated support from the Governmental Logistics Organization, the European main operating bases, and CSC. The results were outstanding: a 40 percent reduction in manpower costs, a 10 percent increase in aircraft availability, and a $300 million decrease in costs to the air force. A big part of the effort was training, including the preparation of the air force personnel for the use of the new processes. The goal was begun at the highest levels of the air force, but it had to be implemented and operated at a local level, so training in new techniques and a thorough understanding of all new policies and procedures were critical to success.

Summary

A key objective for the dieter, losing weight is almost always at the heart of a dietary lifestyle change. In a business setting, it's important to identify the fat and get rid of it. The keys are solid metrics, accurate diagnoses, and a conscientiously applied program.

As lean concepts are applied to the Wall Street diet, the emphasis is placed on the elimination of waste. Doing more with less becomes more than a motto. It becomes a way of doing the processing. An emphasis on ridding the system of bad cholesterol, or non-value-adding activities, is brought to bear as the processes are streamlined as much as possible. To monitor progress, a baseline set of conditions is documented, and charts are used to track the improvements. Above all, the partners in the supply chain work together to make certain lean becomes a way of life across the extended enterprise, and people are involved from end to end, ensuring the body stays lean and does not fall back into former bad habits.

Checklist for Senior Management

☐ Understand that waste can be present in every activity in your enterprise, from inventory to meetings.

☐ Charge your immediate reports to bring you at least one area where the concept could apply because of waste in existing processing.

☐ Establish a time frame in which documented evidence of the causes and elimination of waste are presented.

Checklist for Functional Managers and Diet Champions

☐ Determine whether the actions you ask your team to undertake add value to your customers, team, suppliers, or shareholders.

☐ Select a target area to begin applying the lean concepts.

☐ Organize a lean steering committee, distribute summaries of the concepts, and develop a company-specific interpretation.

☐ Question activities that you feel do not add value.

Stick to Your Diet— Use Quality for Measurement

Many people start a regimen of diet and exercise without a clear vision of what they want to accomplish. Those who want simply to "lose weight" almost invariably fail in the long term. Weight loss as a goal is shortsighted and will often fail to produce long-term benefits. Those who do succeed in becoming fit and those who succeed in quality programs share the same approach: Always start with a clear understanding of the current situation and a clear vision of what you want to accomplish—good health for the individual or the company. This vision inevitably revolves around the following three fundamental needs of dieters:

- They want to become more attractive to themselves and others.
- They want to become more physically fit and active.
- They want to become healthier.

We know that to be successful, dieters must understand the causes of the weight problem. It's not just a matter of eating too much; it's *why* they eat too much. To be successful, they will need to explore the bad habits or causes of the weight problem. The dieters will need to take a new approach to their lifestyle that will require constant attention to all elements until the new, desired lifestyle becomes habitual.

How does quality fit into the Wall Street Diet? Like weight loss only, quality as a goal is shortsighted. Your quality program has to become a part of the fabric of your company and be used to measure and improve your important business goals. It is important to choose the right quality tools for your company and partners. Too much spent on quality and its diminishing returns are almost as bad as not having enough focus on quality.

Adopting the Wall Street Diet allows a company and its partners to start with a clear vision that revolves around where the organization is with respect to the following three fundamental requirements:

- The requirement for quality products/services that customers value
- The need to become more nimble to respond better to market demands
- The need to become leaner to improve the business's health and bottom line

One beauty of the Wall Street Diet is that these quality tools leverage, integrate, and measure the other disciplines—advanced supply chain management, lean enterprise, selective outsourcing, and more. The firm does not have to choose between one and another. In fact, the firm chooses all of them, and the quality program helps you decide the order and the depth of the implementations.

We have positioned quality within the Wall Street Diet to ensure that the right conditions are achieved and operating metrics are used to sustain the diet. This is similar to applying a dietary regimen to remove excess fat from a human body and then keeping it off. Quality should be used to make certain the customer receives what is needed, when it is needed, and at optimum costs and as a mechanism to guarantee the firm and its allies benefit from the effort.

The appropriate quality system is implemented with lean principles and a tool kit of proven advanced supply chain techniques including value stream mapping. Once the link is established between best business processes and the appropriate quality imperatives, members of the emerging value-managed enterprise can increase value for all supply chain constituents.

The most appropriate control system is then used to guarantee that the results of the operating system meet market and customer needs, differentiate the firm and its business allies from competing networks, and prevent the kind of backsliding that is prevalent in fad diets.

BRIEF HISTORY OF THE QUALITY MOVEMENT

Quality has been a business issue since the beginning of commerce. Over the years, the importance of quality has ebbed and flowed depending on market factors, and customers have been disappointed nearly as often as they have been pleased. During the 1950s, when product demand was at unprecedented highs, quality seemed to slip off the radar screen, and customers were often forced to accept whatever passed for a finished product.

Quality as a business imperative was really discovered in the United States in the 1970s, when quality expert W. Edwards Deming was featured on a television special, *If Japan Can, Why Can't We?* This documentary showed how he had helped Japan achieve unusually high levels of quality. He immediately attracted national attention by using statistical process control (SPC) and the need to separate random variations from process variation within control limits as his dogma.

Another American quality specialist, Joseph Juran, further popularized the notion that quality was a key business issue, one that could differentiate a firm and its products. Juran's emphasis was on finding breakthrough achievements on a project-by-project basis. He also emphasized the use of teams to find hidden values in operating systems. He cautioned against an obsession with statistics and technology. The focus must remain, he stressed, on finding new ways to achieve and sustain improved processing. He kept emphasizing throughout his career that the rewards could be enormous if enough breakthroughs were discovered and implemented. He lamented most U.S. management's tolerance of slow and evolutionary progress with quality.

Yet another quality expert, Philip B. Crosby, used an easy, effective style to introduce a terminology and a fourteen-step improvement process that would lead to superior results. His idea was that all quality should be oriented around "doing it right the first time," and he embraced the axiom that the standard should be zero defects—all production made within established standards.

Before Crosby, the general assumption was that guaranteeing quality had to come through inspection, to separate the bad parts from the good. Crosby insisted that doing things wrong made costs skyrocket. He attacked the idea of acceptable quality levels and insisted that following a rigid adherence to quality would not cost a firm any money; it would actually save money.

The quality movement had common elements even as the individual thought leaders emphasized different aspects. Most quality programs include these factors:

- A focus on the system and its processes
- The importance of statistics and the critical role of controlling variation

- The importance of people—especially front-line workers—in building teams and finding solutions
- A goal of delighting the customer through high quality
- A search for "root causes" and a focus on the vital few instead of the urgent many
- A belief that defects can and should be eliminated
- A focus on prevention instead of inspection

Most companies didn't understand that quality has to become part of the corporate lifestyle, instead of a program or process to be bolted on. The Wall Street Diet shows you how to change your corporate lifestyle and embed quality in everything you do.

The selected quality imperative should fit the needs of the customers, the realities of the market, and the firm's ability to recover the costs.

TODAY'S QUALITY: SIX SIGMA SETS A POPULAR BUT DIFFICULT QUALITY GOAL

In essence, Six Sigma is team-based problem solving aimed at reducing process variation through the use of statistical tools. The tactics and tools supporting this concept are primarily intended to improve quality of the product or service by reducing variation around the target value and focusing on activities that are truly important to customers. The firm must select an appropriate quality level that satisfies customer needs and allows the firm to operate profitably. This level becomes the appropriate sigma level.

Exhibit 5.1 presents a familiar bell-shaped curve that includes the entire variation in a process or the entire customer (from upper to lower statistical limits) tolerance requirements, with three sigma represented within that curve. The problem compounds when variation this broad is combined with parts or other processes with a similar variation. The compounded variations, all within tolerance, might make the product assembly

EXHIBIT 5.1   Three Sigma Distribution

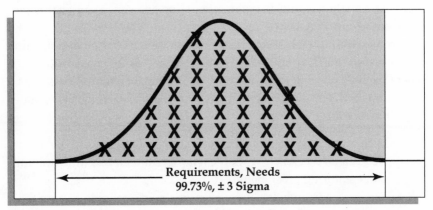

Requirements, Needs
99.73%, ± 3 Sigma

or total effort inferior or downright unacceptable to internal and external customers. A second problem is that any shift in the center of the variation will result in a tail of the distribution being beyond the customer needs, and waste (scrap or rework) will be produced.

If the variation is reduced to the Six Sigma target, the spread will look more like the curve within a curve depicted in Exhibit 5.2, where the variation consumes only half of the customer needs and requirements. With much less variation—from, say, three sigma (99.73 percent accuracy) to six sigma (99.99999998 percent accuracy)—processes and parts work and fit together much better. Should the center of the variation shift slightly,

EXHIBIT 5.2   Six Sigma Distribution

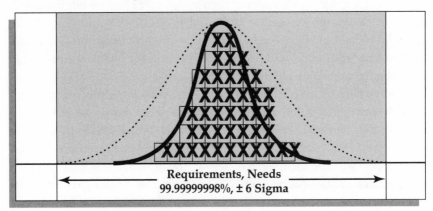

Requirements, Needs
99.99999998%, ± 6 Sigma

acceptable products will still be produced. For those in service organizations, less variation results in better scheduling and consistent quality performance to customers.

Six Sigma in its purest form requires a rather extensive organization and infrastructure. Its popularity has been restricted to large corporations where the high costs of initiating and maintaining such processes can be better absorbed. For example, the typical Six Sigma organization includes these individuals:

- Executives and champions who charter and motivate action teams
- Dedicated "black belt" experts, who spend their full time training and mentoring green belts
- Part-time "green belts," who learn statistical techniques from the black belts and lead teams in reducing variation and solving problems
- Team members who work on reducing variations and solving problems

The Six Sigma teams meet and work regularly until the goals established by the executives and champions have been met.

Small firms often find the Six Sigma bureaucracy too expensive for the potential gains. They frequently turn to outside consulting resources to train and facilitate Six Sigma–type projects. If you are in this position, we recommend that you examine your supply chain partners for Six Sigma expertise and leverage those activities. After all, it is to their benefit as well.

In the 1990s, toward the end of the Jack Welch era, General Electric discovered Six Sigma. With firms such as 3M and Honeywell, it went in search of more improvement, with the aid of black belt helpers, who were specially trained in the concepts. This move brought attention to the concept on a national scale, and a large number of large organizations began adopting the Six Sigma techniques.

Today, the bar has been raised with both quality and Six Sigma. With the customer in a much better position to select between competing sources, the offering that is most attractive gets the business. Quality is now viewed as the ante in the business game, and enhanced process improvements become the means of setting the organization apart from its competitors. Without acceptable quality, however, nothing else matters because customers will not buy. With acceptable quality, customers can look beyond the product to compare offerings that include such things as price, delivery, and service. Exemplary quality, however, can often overcome concerns for price and delivery issues.

UNDERSTANDING THE QUALITY ENTERPRISE

The questions, from the vantage of the Wall Street Diet, become, What is the right quality system for your business? How do you merge quality with lean manufacturing to achieve the necessary level of quality performance while helping decrease costs and improve customer satisfaction? For the value-managed enterprise we are considering, the answers mean we must find the system that raises quality to the highest level compatible with customer needs, without bankrupting the firm through the effort. It also means blending quality and lean productivity into a coherent business philosophy and methodology.

As with any diet, it is critical that we know where we are and where we want to be so the gaps can be established and the proper diet and exercise selected to reach our objectives. Exhibits 5.3 through 5.5 help identify where we are, where we need to be, and how we can use quality as an enabler of the organizational strategic objectives. In each of the exhibits, we see three axes of attention arrayed with corresponding quality objectives: conformance quality, delivery performance, and total cost. As you proceed through the exhibits, we encourage you to recognize the need to exceed customer's conformance requirements and evaluate your firm's ability to do so.

Your organization will want to consider that industry leaders uniquely dominate their most important competitive axis to gain a sustainable advantage. Also bear in mind that regardless of your internal opinions, customers are the ones who really define the minimum acceptable levels for the three strategic objectives outlined. As customer expectations and competitive offerings change, your relative position in each of these objectives can change.

To start your organization on its quality path toward greater health, use the following exercise, which begins in Exhibit 5.3. Ask, "How does our *conformance quality* compare with the minimum acceptable level, with what our competitors have achieved, and with what our key customers demand?" Evaluate and record your conformance quality along the vertical

EXHIBIT 5.3 Hierarchy of Operational Requirements—Conformance Quality

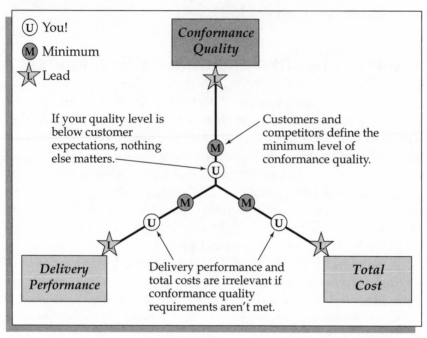

continuum against where your organization is positioned with respect to customer expectations and competitive pressures. To help with this evaluation, we find it is very useful to include reviews with key customers to verify perceptions. If your quality level is below customer expectations, for example, nothing else matters—delivery performance and total costs are irrelevant if conformance quality requirements are not being met.

Having evaluated where your firm is with respect to conformance quality, next evaluate your *delivery performance* against customer requirements and competitive offerings, as illustrated in Exhibit 5.4. Again, be careful to identify where the organization stands with respect to delivery performance on the lower-left strategic objective.

When that position has been established, evaluate your performance with respect to *total cost*, as shown on the lower-right leg in Exhibit 5.5, and place your rating on that strategic objective.

At the end of this exercise, you've created a graphic depiction of the three strategic competitive objectives, and your organization knows

EXHIBIT 5.4 Hierarchy of Operational Requirements—Delivery Performance

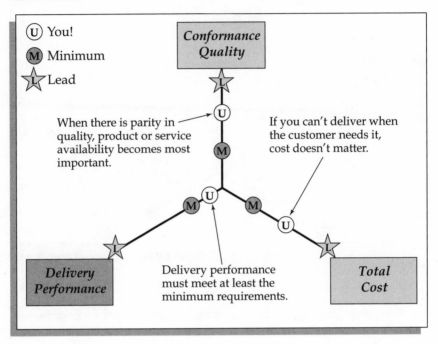

where improvement is necessary. You will have identified where action must be taken to gain dominance or to shore up weaknesses. Three factors come into play:

- Many companies find that outstanding conformance quality, delivery performance, and total cost are not mutually exclusive. Attention to quality leads to better performance in all three areas.
- Use of the productivity profile technique (explained in Chapter 6) will show how all three areas can be improved simultaneously, as the profiles will indicate virtually all weaknesses in current processing.
- With the proper tactics and techniques, we find all three factors can be improved.

This is a crucial exercise. Your diet objectives will be determined by the outcome of the effort. Equally important, the specific diet and exercises needed to bring you a lasting competitive advantage will be

EXHIBIT 5.5 Hierarchy of Operational Requirements—Total Cost

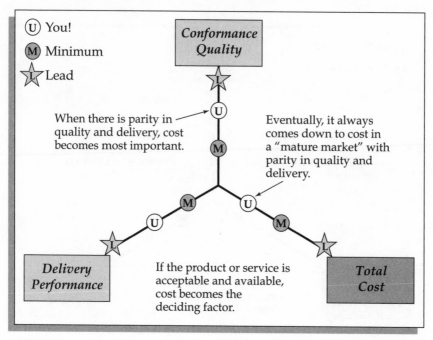

determined by what this exercise demonstrates. If you misdiagnose, the wrong diet and exercise may be prescribed, and you will never reach the healthy state you desire.

LINKING QUALITY WITH LEAN CONCEPTS

The next step in the Wall Street Diet is to develop a balanced approach that links lean, Six Sigma, and other appropriate tools and techniques to achieve the desired objectives. This is much like the balanced approach of dieting and exercise to become fit. Many people try dieting, but without exercise, the body just adjusts the metabolism downward to conserve calories and thwart weight loss. Many people exercise, but without dieting or adjusting the lifestyle, exercise alone usually is not enough to lose weight. Similarly, the integrated approach we are suggesting includes lean, supply chain, quality, and selective outsourcing in a balanced approach to improving the health and appearance of your business.

The underlying idea is to achieve near-perfection within a lean/quality manufacturing or service environment. So what exactly is the correct quality standard in that context? If Six Sigma is merged with lean productivity, what kind of results can you anticipate? Within the bounds of the Wall Street Diet, we define *lean Six Sigma* as *a rigorous problem-solving methodology, designed to assist with total elimination of waste while instilling an ethic of continuous process improvement and variation reduction across the end-to-end supply chain.*

Much like lean thinking, quality is applied as a concept, tool kit, management philosophy, and way of doing business. Root cause analysis becomes an imperative, as does team problem solving. Working on the premises that all processes have some variability and that variability has a cause, the teams search out the few causes that are generally at the root of most problems. To the degree that those causes can be understood, they also can be controlled. Process improvement is then introduced to bring those processes under control. This technique applies regardless of the business, the processes, or the people involved.

Exhibit 5.6 illustrates the kind of connection we are advocating. Here we see the characteristics of a properly applied Six Sigma system laid next to similar characteristics of lean manufacturing. Now the participants can see the linkage and elaborate on the specifics of an action plan based on

EXHIBIT 5.6   Six Sigma and Lean Manufacturing

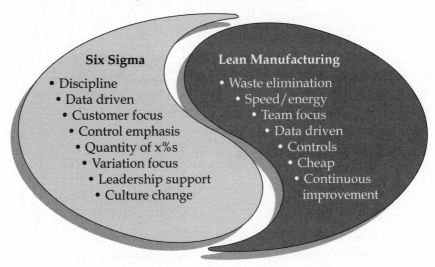

Six Sigma
- Discipline
- Data driven
- Customer focus
- Control emphasis
- Quantity of x%s
- Variation focus
- Leadership support
- Culture change

Lean Manufacturing
- Waste elimination
- Speed/energy
- Team focus
- Data driven
- Controls
- Cheap
- Continuous improvement

accomplishing the features illustrated. We advise customizing this chart for your specific firm and its network participants.

Next, the organization takes a broader view of what is being created and, using Exhibit 5.7 as a guide, prepares for lean Six Sigma governance. As shown, a joint governance board—to determine vision, strategy, plans, and objectives—is advisable, especially to establish the critical problems requiring some change in process capability. You will recall this is the chart we discussed in Chapter 4 (Exhibit 4.6) when we discussed integrating lean enterprise concepts across multiple firms.

The linkage is completed when the lean/quality effort extends across the end-to-end supply chain process.

EXHIBIT 5.7 Building the Lean/Quality Enterprise

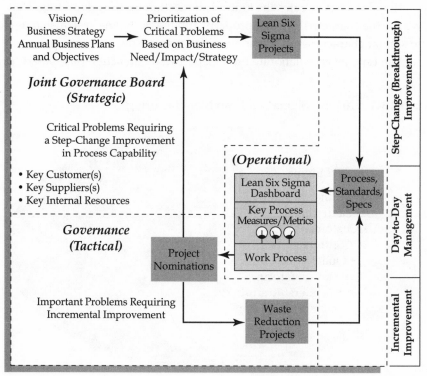

A tactical arm is also necessary to make sure the important problems receive attention and are eliminated. The operational group then sets up some kind of measuring technique, such as a lean Six Sigma dashboard, to track changes from the as-is state to the improved could-be state of operating conditions.

APPLYING QUALITY TO SUPPLY CHAIN

Similar to the process used in Chapter 4 with lean techniques, we need to bring the best quality techniques and practices forward under the supply chain umbrella. Then we go through each of the five levels of the maturity model to see how quality becomes a positive factor—perhaps starting with team problem solving and root cause analysis in Level 1. Understanding of other tools (e.g., failure modes and effect analysis) comes into play in Level 2. Then we move into collaborative problem-solving actions across the network in Levels 3 and 4, where quality is applied to remove bottlenecks and eliminate higher operating costs. Finally, in Level 5, we should link quality with network connectivity to share best practices and use measurements to make certain any improvements are sustained—no backsliding allowed.

CONTEMPORARY BUSINESS MODEL

Mike Wells, president of King Machine, demonstrates this broad perspective as he relates his experiences with a quality effort, choosing to apply an ISO-based quality system for his business needs. Established in the 1980s, the ISO (the International Organization for Standardization) quality standards have achieved great recognition in several industries, most notably the automotive and aerospace industries. Developed by an international standards body and focusing on operations, the ISO quality standards have helped many companies. Again, a real first step is determining which quality system is most appropriate for your company, just as Wells did.

King Machine manufactures and repairs tire molds for tire manufacturing companies. In 2001, the company had three plants in North Carolina and one in Akron, Ohio. In mid-2001, it began the development of its ISO 9001:2000 Quality Management System. Wells acknowledges, "We did not start the process because of customer pressure, but rather because we believed it would be good for our business."

It was not the best of times for those in the tire mold industry. Business was slow, and tire companies were not developing as many new tires as in previous years. Customers were in a position to demand more and pay less. Many of the firm's competitors had gone or were going out of business, and the competition for the business that remained was fierce. Fortunately, King Machine already had a reputation for quality, and with all other factors being equal, it was often the supplier of choice. Unfortunately, however, the way the company had achieved its high outgoing quality was both expensive and time-consuming. Consequently, King often found itself facing a competitive disadvantage.

As the firm studied the situation, it realized that the level of quality that made King the envy of the tire mold industry was achieved by spending too much time redoing and reworking. In other words, King always took the time to get the job done right—but not the first time. The end product was good, but because of the necessary changes to get things right, the overall processes took too long and cost too much.

Further study showed King had the right tools and people but lacked the manufacturing and management systems and processes. King needed to improve its systems if the company was to survive in the long run. The decision was subsequently made that quality would be the ingredient to add to the already-high manufacturing and delivery processing capabilities. ISO 9001:2000 was selected as the appropriate vehicle.

The ISO 9001:2000 standards had recently been published, and King's management concluded that it provided the model to achieve the much-needed process improvements. At that time, the company was more interested in following the ISO requirements to better its business than it was with gaining certification. In fact, throughout the implementation, certification was viewed as a by-product of implementation rather than the objective.

Current employees did not have extensive ISO experience. In addition, many of King's employees had spent their entire career with the company and had limited experience with other systems and processes. The company decided it needed professional help in developing and implementing the ISO 9001:2000 system; Bill Houser was selected for the assignment. Management believed it was absolutely critical that King Machine receive the most benefit from the ISO installation, and Houser's philosophies and methods met the company's views and needs of an implementation aimed at improving the business.

The effort began in June 2001 with what Houser terms "the push-pull phase." Push-pull starts with recognition that it takes a great deal of effort to develop a quality management system that is compliant with ISO 9001:2000. This effort can come from two sources:

- Forces that are pushing—usually negative forces
- Forces that are pulling—the more desired positive forces

The combination of these must be enough to provide support and sustain motivation.

As each plant began its ISO 9001:2000 development, the management team went through the push-pull process, listing both the forces pushing and those pulling the organization toward ISO 9000. The president's name appeared in the push column! While pressures pushing an organization like King may force development of a system, they will not force development beyond a "minimum system." Pull forces, on the other hand, provide insight into how the system should be designed, as well as organizational and individual incentives to develop and implement a system providing the kind of improvement needed. King kept the original push-pull chart as a reference against progress. It has been laminated, and if you visit the conference room in Charlotte today, you will find it framed and signed.

As the development proceeded, the management at King constantly reminded themselves that improvement was the overriding objective. As they dealt with each requirement in the standard, they did not ask, "What is necessary to meet the standard?" Rather, they asked two questions:

- Is this requirement reasonable? The answer was always "Yes!" aside from those areas being excluded.
- What is the best way for King Machine to meet the requirement? The team recognized that they wanted a system that met the firm's needs first and the standard second.

It is interesting to note that every time the team went through the soul-searching, fussing, and feuding necessary to find the best processes to meet needs, those processes met the ISO requirements as well.

As development of the ISO 9001:2000 management system progressed, King selected its registrar. The certification audit for the first two plants was in the latter part of 2002, and all went well. The auditors were very complimentary and very thorough. The second two plants followed in 2003 with the same results.

But that is only the beginning of the story. The ISO 9001:2000 quality management system is alive, well, and still growing. King's objective is to be recognized as the company that produces the highest-quality tire molds, delivered more quickly and at competitive prices—the differentiating characteristic of the King network. As stated earlier, outgoing quality has always been very high, but it was achieved through excessive reworking that played havoc with quick delivery and costs. Crucial to further progress was recognizing that tire manufacturers differentiate their mold selections based on quick response and that the time line from design to tires in the marketplace has never been shorter. To support its customers, King needed a lean technique—to continuously implement ways to reduce mold lead time from drawings to mold delivery.

Shortened lead times get tires in the marketplace sooner, while allowing the tire manufacturers to spend more time designing, testing, perfecting, and making marketing decisions before committing to mold purchase. Therefore, shortening the delivery cycle became a strategic objective for King Machine to support its customers and gain new business. Many things were done to shorten delivery cycle time.

For example, the company started measuring its cost of nonconformance—the cost generated by problems that are slowing down, stopping, and backing up tire molds as they progress through the system. Once identified, these costs needed to be eliminated. The CAPAR (Corrective and Preventive Action Request) system is now used to solve the problems exposed by the cost of nonconformance. The firm has become relentless in this pursuit—of discovery of problems as well as their resolution—because it can improve both costs and delivery if the problems that contribute to the cost of nonconformance are eliminated.

The president personally reviews all CAPARs. The company does not like ongoing problems, and the only way to root them out is to recognize they exist and then find ways to prevent their recurrence. The CAPAR system does that, and although some people might get concerned when they see a problem, the president gets concerned when they *stop* seeing problems. For example, about a year ago, Wells noticed that the number of CAPARs being generated was falling off. This meant to him that the CAPAR-related improvements would be slowing down. This situation was discussed during a management review, and it was decided that the senior management of each plant must generate at least one "management CAPAR" per month—a current problem, potential problem, or continual improvement that must be recognized so it can be resolved. Wells polices this requirement carefully, and it has been very successful.

The management CAPARs technique has been so successful that King is currently implementing the same requirement for various plant departments. They are generating more CAPARs than ever. Since these CAPARs are being resolved, further improvement is continuing. Wells attends all management reviews, which have proven to be critically important. These reviews are all-day working sessions during which significant decisions are made. Important changes in direction and some of the best continual improvement projects have come from these reviews.

According to Wells, "Implementing the quality management system is not the only thing we've been doing to better serve our customers. Some new equipment has been purchased. We became more vertically integrated by adding a foundry (currently implementing an ISO 9001:2000 system). The results of implementing the quality management system and our other initiatives are that our customer base has expanded. We have moved from a second-tier to top-tier supplier with one of our customers. We continually get high marks from our customers for our quality management system. (Incidentally, certification to ISO 9001:2000 is now becoming a requirement for tire mold producers.) Our volumes, market share, and efficiency are all up, and our mold lead times are dropping dramatically. [In 2004,] we consolidated two of our North Carolina plants into much larger and better laid-out facilities to better service our customers. The ISO system helped the move go flawlessly—we didn't miss a shipment."

The ISO 9001:2000 system and other changes have benefited King's customers in the speed with which expedited/quick-response molds are produced on a regular and consistent basis. Lead times for expedited molds have been reduced more than 40 percent over the past year. The firm has lessened the lead time needed from drawings to finished product—a 13 percent reduction for both expedited and standard molds in 2004. This improvement has given King's customers a competitive advantage in being first to market with their tires.

SUMMARY

Before dieters can begin the regimen that would yield the greatest success, they need a clear idea of what to accomplish. They also need to understand the habits of a lifetime that caused them to become overweight, out of shape, and unhealthy. In most cases, several bad habits are at fault, which is why a lifestyle change is needed. The successful dieter needs to combine several approaches. Accurate and reliable measurements will be needed to be able to choose effectively.

The Wall Street Diet will not be totally effective and lead to optimized operating conditions and new revenues unless there is a strong commitment to a quality aspect within the diet execution. In this chapter, we have considered the linkage between quality and three value disciplines. We positioned quality as a key element in gaining the desired position in all three. Moreover, we have shown how three similar but distinct efforts to improve conformance quality, delivery performance, and total cost will solidify the firm's ability to use quality, not just to meet minimum customer requirements but to improve costs and productivity as well.

Quality is also used to ensure that the gains made are not lost. Consider the analogy of a man climbing a rope. He may have great physical strength in his arms and be able to climb the rope, but most athletes will secure their position on the rope by wrapping their legs around the rope so that they don't slide back. Adhering to quality standards, particularly the ISO standards, is like locking legs around the rope. Such a move will ensure that the higher quality and productivity are sustained and that the firm and its allies do not slip back to former unhealthy positions.

CHECKLIST FOR SENIOR MANAGEMENT

☐ Understand that quality is a powerful tool when used alone, but it is even more powerful when combined with other approaches. Seek the widest application, always looking for ways to integrate quality into the fabric of your business.

☐ Know when you may be part of the problem and how to keep the right pressure on in the right areas.

☐ Insist that your direct reports bring you a viable plan for the appropriate quality standard as part of the diet.

☐ Turn the orientation of your business into a pull mode, focusing on satisfying the customer.

CHECKLIST FOR FUNCTIONAL MANAGERS AND DIET CHAMPIONS

☐ Identify your "Hierarchy of Operational Requirements" using the examples of Exhibits 5.3 through 5.5. Survey customers and key players within your organization to arrive at a consensus.

☐ Establish your goals to provide an ongoing incentive to work toward the appropriate goals.

☐ Use the quality analytical tools to identify where the organization is and establish goals with respect to quality, delivery, and cost.

☐ Brush up your quality skills. They will be useful throughout your entire supply chain.

Chart Your Health—Use Productivity Profiling to Target Gains

Dieters often have had an initial physical exam, and baselines were created. They probably have tracked weight loss on the bathroom scale and noticed how well their clothes fit.

While these actions are quick and easy indicators, they may not be accurate or reliable. For example, muscle cells in the body weigh more than fat cells; therefore, when dieters lose fat and build muscle through exercise, they may weigh more but be in better shape. Specific and accurate body measurements may tell dieters what they need to know. It is absolutely essential to have the right tools to get the right measurements.

At the same time, we cannot forget the value of before and after pictures. In business, there are plenty of "quick snapshot" measurements that point out the general direction but do not serve as good diagnostic tools.

Using the right tools makes every part of the Wall Street Diet easier. We pause in this chapter to examine two very powerful tools: the horn of uncertainty and productivity profiling. The Wall Street Diet has emphasized using applications across business units, the firm, and the enterprise network. Not every area will respond as quickly and completely to these applications. These tools will help create a common understanding of success, and they can be used for both manufacturing and services applications. They are also the keys to the ultimate success of the diet.

Bringing an organization to peak and lasting performance in terms of cost, productivity, and quality is the greatest challenge facing organizations today. The will to achieve this level is not enough. There needs to be a vision clearly showing how the lean and fit organization can be achieved. And, the right tools and approaches must be in place.

As we have analyzed numerous companies and industries, we find enormous opportunities to create better processing even after prior concentrated improvement efforts. More fat remains in spite of previous diets. The improvement opportunity centers on finding the hidden wastes and the presence of non-value-adding work that still exists across the extended enterprise. These elements are much greater than imagined in virtually every instance we have explored. The firms just have not reached conditions of total enterprise optimization (TEO).

DIAGNOSIS SHOWS THE POTENTIAL FOR IMPROVEMENT

Like a medical checkup, diagnosis exposes the specific gap between your current organizational health and what is needed in an ever more competitive world. Once the specific health gap is established, techniques to close the gap can be identified and implemented. The right measurements can be sobering. It is like telling a person who has reduced body weight from 300 pounds to 225 pounds that the chart indicates, for height and age, 185 is the better number.

In this chapter, we present proven methods and tools for achieving the desired future state of performance—correct weight and conditions of health—instead of the current obese operating conditions. Closing the gap will inevitably require integrating the best practices and process activities within the organization's four walls, and working with the closest partners across the extended business network. The effort should quickly extend over the network to discover and deploy proven solutions, regardless of which partner developed the improvement.

A paralyzing attitude we commonly see is that a firm believes it has done what can be done and cannot progress further without significant capital investment. Throwing money at the problem is not the answer. Using profiling techniques, a firm can determine how much waste or non-value exists within a process and, eventually, a supply chain system; how much potential output has not been achieved; and how much further productivity and quality are possible with a particular business network. These techniques can be applied to any process within any business.

MATCHING SUPPLY WITH DEMAND

The first tool dismantles a major barrier to better asset utilization and efficient supply chain processing. Most problems within a supply chain would evaporate if forecasted demand was 100 percent accurate and/or supply chain lead times were near zero. In that ideal world, the responding system would always be providing what was needed at the time of need, without extra supplies. Unfortunately, the real business world is characterized by uncertainty about demand and is filled with long lead times—typical supply chain nemeses.

Matching demand signals, capacity, and lead times, and doing a better job of demand management, have become important contemporary business issues. Exhibit 6.1 illustrates these forecasting and lead time problems. The vertical line represents volume; the horizontal line represents the "best estimate" forecast over time, as it extends from the present on the left to the future to the right.

Often, the forecasted volume will vary up and down in future periods, but for the sake of simplicity, the chart's forecasted volume is constant from the present to the distant future. If we can be certain about one thing, it is that the actual demand will not match the best forecast. As time progresses, the actual demand might be higher or lower than the best

EXHIBIT 6.1   The Horn of Uncertainty—Effect of Long Lead Times and Imprecise Forecasts

Forecasting "Horn of Uncertainty"

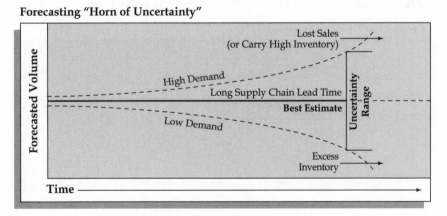

estimate. The further into the future we go, the more the error opens exponentially, producing what we term the *horn of uncertainty*.

When we consider the typical long supply chain lead time, the difference between the "uncertainty range" of actual sales and the best estimate is very large. If the sales volume comes in at the high demand side of the horn of uncertainty, there will be excessive overtime, expedited delivery costs along the supply chain, and, inevitably, lost sales and upset customers. These are opportunities for competitors with available capacity.

On the other hand, if the sales volume comes in at the low demand side, there will be excess inventory that, if it becomes obsolete, can present very bad conditions for a business, often leading to price reductions to cover the effect of the poor forecasts. Inventory also costs money. The bloated conditions at both the high and low demand sides of the horn of uncertainty reduce competitiveness.

The *uncertainty range* can be reduced in two ways. One way is to improve forecasting; the second is to reduce the cycle time so that we do not need to forecast so far into the future.

Examining forecasting first, we can see in Exhibit 6.2 that a reduction to the uncertainty range is possible if we improve forecasting accuracy. Forecasting is a key component in supply chains, greatly affecting the overall performance of the supply chain and contributing to the excesses and wastes. Marketing information from a variety of database sources, including historical trends, is merged with withdrawals from warehouses

EXHIBIT 6.2   Effect of Improved Forecasts and Lead Times

Forecasting "Horn of Uncertainty"

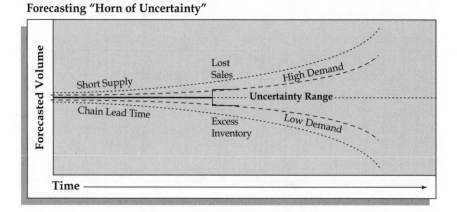

and actual sales. Sales personnel are constantly queried about customer demands and any unanticipated changes in the pattern of their purchases. Planning and forecasting departments do all they can to analyze the data and present reasonable estimates of what can be expected in the way of actual orders. Better demand forecasting or demand management becomes the end game. Unfortunately, our experiences show that firms can vary from lows of 30 to 40 percent forecast accuracy to highs of 75 to 80 percent, making the objective of absolute accuracy very elusive.

Complete forecast accuracy is never going to be reached, but we can reduce the amount of uncertainty. The secret is working closer with all of the constituents in the extended network, especially the key customers. When tighter relationships are forged, we have seen forecast accuracies dramatically improved much like that depicted in Exhibit 6.2, where participants have reduced the uncertainty range.

The effort starts by considering the alternatives to accepting poor incoming information and working with customers and suppliers to match demand with supply with greater precision. Together, the business partners look for ways to minimize the variability, or the volatility, of the accepted forecast. One focus is the inherent demand variability caused by natural consumption factors. The other is the artificial variability introduced by market aberrations and supply chain practices such as promotions, sales contest, special events, and so forth. (The route to better forecasting is described in detail in Chapter 5 of *Using Models to Improve Supply Chains* by Poirier [2003].)

As also depicted in Exhibit 6.2, the second approach to reducing the uncertainty range is to cut the supply chain lead time by trimming the non-value-adding fat. As the time frames across the supply chain shorten, the system becomes more responsive, and we can commit to production later with a smaller uncertainty range. Within the internal operations, bills of material become more accurate with better input from more reliable sources. Advanced planning and scheduling are in place and used to show what is being planned and what will be going through manufacturing. All raw materials, work in process, and finished goods can be viewed and taken into account as inventory levels are determined and warehouse space is allocated.

On the purchasing side, key suppliers are hard at work providing the available-to-supply information and warning of any constraints in their systems. Their inventories are managed in sync with the demand signals being sent upstream. Order status is online, as well as information on engineering and manufacturing changes affecting supply. The firm's supplier relationship management system matches purchase orders with the demand signals and manages supply chain requirements. Inbound logistics has become as important as outbound logistics as the supply planners know where everything is at any time and can make forecast adjustments based on any expected interruptions.

To increase revenues and control costs, we must simultaneously improve forecasting and shorten lead times.

Of course, as illustrated in Exhibit 6.2, the best way to reduce the uncertainty range is by simultaneously improving forecasting and reducing the supply chain lead time. When these two factors are combined, we start to move to a controllable range of uncertainty. A reasonable or manageable exception-handling system can deal with the smaller demand swings within the tighter uncertainty range—conditions desired by the Wall Street Diet. Productivity profiling—our next topic—has proven very useful to both reduce lead times and hone a flexible supply chain that can cope with inevitable demand swings within the narrower horn of uncertainty.

PRODUCTIVITY PROFILING

Productivity profiling has proven to be very effective in identifying both the current and the ideal process health state, which exposes the gap and motivates improvement. The results often shock a typical organization into understanding just how much further potential improvement still exists. With the help of productivity profiling, we show how a firm and its network allies can move to the higher levels of the supply chain maturity model and develop the desired lean body conditions of a value-managed enterprise.

Profiling creates a simultaneous focus on the total quality, productivity, cost, and waste reduction opportunities that still exist in an operating system. This then leads to using the Wall Street Diet to eliminate the root causes of problems and raise the firm and network to industry-best levels. The results are impressive:

- Lowering of costs by as much as 15 to 20 percent or more
- Reduction of delay times by 50 percent or more
- Higher quality—reaching the appropriate sigma level
- Increased asset and capacity utilization, forestalling major capital expansion projects
- Quicker and better setups and changeovers, resulting in greater flexibility and responsiveness to market and customer needs
- Integrated plans of action that yield a seamless response to key customers

Productivity profiling is a tool we developed and perfected through experiences in numerous companies and industries. The tool compares a utopian view of a business process against the current state to provide motivation for improvement, insight as to the degree of improvement opportunity possible, and identification of specific areas most in need of improvement. The utopian state should not be viewed as a complex issue but a simple description of what the capacity or output of a function or process would be if everything were done under perfect conditions. It's like viewing a manufacturing process as if the machines were running at peak capacity for the full time that they were scheduled and crewed for operation, or the output of a billing department that made no mistakes for the full eight hours the employees were processing bills. It's like the dieter hanging two pictures side by side, the current and an idealized body shape, as an inspiration to stick with a diet and exercise regimen.

Productivity profiling is equally applicable to manufacturing and service organizations. Whether dealing with a bank process, a hospital operation, a distribution process, a retail system, an office function, or a manufacturing process, productivity profiling begins with *process mapping*. A process to be improved is selected and a map—a detailed, graphic depiction—of the process developed. The map describes all of the steps in that process and their interactions, so that the critical path determining the cycle time for the entire process can be identified.

Depicting a typical system productivity profile, Exhibit 6.3 has three separate but integrally related elements. At the top is the critical path for a manufacturing process map. In the middle, the steps and actual times being taken to complete each step on the critical path are plotted to show the value-adding and non-value-adding steps and their relationship. In the value-adding steps, the part is actually being worked on or transformed

EXHIBIT 6.3 Typical System Productivity Profile

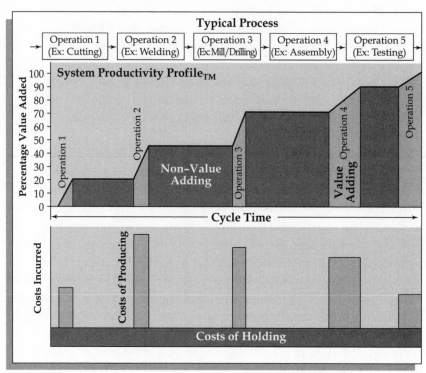

into a more valuable component or assembly (or value is added to a service function). The non-value-adding steps take resources but add no value, as when the components are moved, stored, counted, inspected, accumulated into larger lots, and so forth. These steps are shown as the horizontal line segments. This effort will typically show that while some time is spent adding value by performing the identified operations, the majority of time is spent in the non-value area, uselessly stretching the overall cycle time and costs.

As seen in the lower portion of Exhibit 6.3, the costs for the value-adding steps occur in bursts of activity, while the costs for the non-value-adding activities are relatively constant during the entire cycle time. The periods of significantly higher expenditure correspond to the value-adding portions of the process, which involve relatively intense activity.

In both manufacturing and service organizations, we find the value-adding time is typically less than 10 percent of the total time available and

EXHIBIT 6.4   Profiles Identify the Process Steps to Study

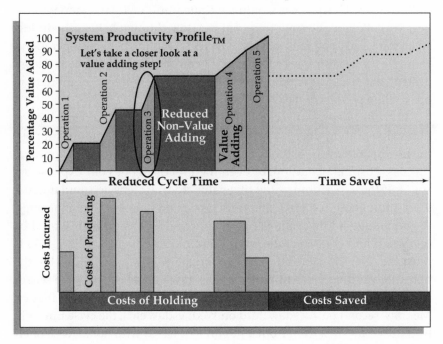

is highly variable. The other 90 percent causes longer cycle times and an increased "cost of holding." Overall costs are higher. Reducing the non-value-adding time both saves time and cuts costs, but it requires streamlining the overall processing, cutting down any identified waiting time, moving to continuous flow, and entirely eliminating as many non-value-adding steps as possible.

As shown in Exhibit 6.4, it is not uncommon to see the value-adding portion go from under 10 percent to a consistent 50 percent or more as the non-value-adding steps are reduced or eliminated. Fortunately, reducing the non-value-adding steps does not typically require large capital expenditures. Similar to the system productivity profile, the process productivity profile like Exhibit 6.5 presents a graphical view of a production operation to identify and target process improvement opportunities.

For example, when working with a client operating a large metal rolling mill, we were able to both improve customer response and free up working capital quickly and with minimal investment. The client's process map showed that the firm progressively rolled the metal ever thinner and then annealed the metal in a furnace to resoften it before rolling again. This process would continue until the final material thickness was attained. By smoothing out the flow through better scheduling, smaller lot sizes, and fans to hasten the metal cooling between operations, the cycle time was improved by over 30 percent, the mill area was decongested, and working capital was freed up by the removal of more than one million pounds of metal inventory.

In the service sector, scheduling improvements will often bring the non-value-adding steps down dramatically. As an illustration, suppose the five operations in Exhibits 6.3 and 6.4 were for a bank loan approval process, hospital operation, or even the processing of your expense account. If those performing the five value-adding steps accumulated the work throughout the week and only processed it on Monday mornings, the non-value-adding time between value-adding operations would be one week, and the cycle time would be a minimum of four weeks. As is often the case, the value-adding times might be only a few hours, but the non-value-adding times turn into weeks. If we merely change the schedule so the operations are done on progressive days of the week (first on Monday, second on Tuesday, third on Wednesday, etc.), the cycle time will be reduced by 75 percent from a month to a week, with no increase of effort on anyone's part. Of course, if we made the process truly "flow," we could potentially bring the cycle time down from a month to minutes.

Process productivity profiling focuses attention on the area of greatest improvement need: setup losses, inertial losses, speed losses, downtime losses, and quality losses.

The value-adding steps also contain a great deal of fat that needs to be eliminated. In Exhibit 6.5, we begin to concentrate on one of the value-adding steps from the system productivity profile and the associated losses. As can be seen in the process productivity profile of this exhibit, any process contains five potential losses: setup losses, inertial losses, speed losses, downtime losses, and quality losses. We will examine each of the five potential loss areas in detail.

Setup Losses. At the beginning of a production run, the process must be set up for the next product to be made or for the next service to be pro-

EXHIBIT 6.5   Five Process Losses

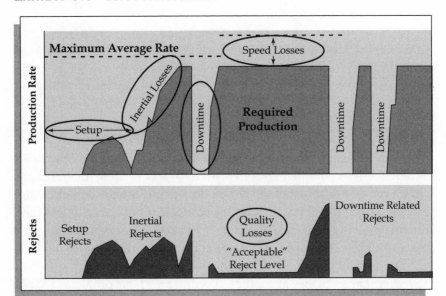

vided. Typically setups or changeovers take longer than they should, and defects, such as setup scrap in preparation materials, result.

As Exhibit 6.5 shows, setup consists of two distinct areas: tool change and adjustment. *Tool change* is the time needed to actually change the tooling, and the *adjustment period* is that time taken to make the necessary adjustments to produce the first good part. By definition, setup is complete when the first good product is produced. Therefore, as seen in the bottom portion of the exhibit, while the setup is being adjusted, all product is defective until the first good part is produced and the setup is complete. Obviously, when the adjustment is made quickly and well, fewer defective parts will be produced.

Inertial Losses.   Long setups with excessive setup scrap are not the only losses in a production process. The setup that produces one good part is often not the setup that will produce good product at full running rates. Therefore, further refinement is often needed to bring the process to the optimum running rate, which produces what we call *inertial losses*—those losses associated with bringing the production up to running rate. The bottom portion of the exhibit reflects the defective product produced during this period. While we find a great deal of variation in inertial losses, we have seen many situations where inertial losses have exceeded the setup-related losses.

Rate or Speed Losses. As we move further into the production process, we find a third loss—rate or speed losses. Processes are often run at less than the optimal speed, usually due to artificially imposed quality and waste constraints. Generally speaking, the actual running rate is determined by the production of some "acceptable" level of quality, because the operators are concerned that above the established running rate, excessive defects and/or machine jams may result. The definition of this "acceptable" level of quality is often arbitrary and variable. Interestingly, while a conventional cost of quality report will pick up the cost of the defects produced, it will not pick up the cost of lost productivity resulting from maintaining an acceptable quality level. We have seen these speed losses as high as 30 percent of the machine's rated output speed.

Downtime Losses. Once at running speed, we find our problems are not over since equipment often experiences downtime interruptions, as illustrated in Exhibit 6.5. Downtime in a typical process represents a major loss of productivity and delay in producing product (or delivering a service). During these interruptions, the labor and capital investment are still being used, but no product is being produced—a major loss we often see in the 20 percent of total capacity range.

Quality Losses. Immediately prior to the downtime, a dramatic increase in the defect rate typically occurs. The process "going out of adjustment" and producing defects is, after all, what often causes downtime. Inertial losses are also experienced as the equipment is brought back up to running speed. Again, while the defects appear in a cost-of-quality report, the productivity losses associated with the downtime normally do not.

The defective portion of the production run has to be rejected to ensure the integrity of the outgoing product. Exhibit 6.6 reflects this sorting effort and the additional production necessary to make up for the product rejected. The objective of this high-cost and non-value-adding sort of effort is to remove the entire defective product without rejecting any of the acceptable products. Perfect sorting is almost never achieved, and acceptable product is often rejected while defective product is accepted, resulting in increased costs and customer complaints. To supply the required

EXHIBIT 6.6 Actual Results with Reject Compensation

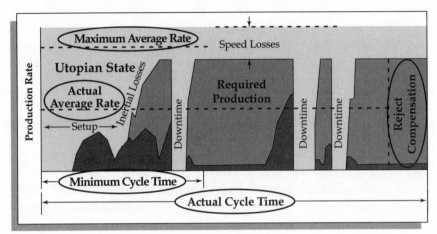

order quantity, production needs to be continued to make up for the rejected product, as illustrated at the right of Exhibit 6.6. This product is doubly expensive: We have already paid to produce it once, and now we are paying to produce it a second time.

The background of Exhibit 6.6 presents the utopian state. The area under the curve, representing production, is the same as the profile in the foreground. The utopian state shows that if we take the minimum setup time combined with an instantaneous rise to the maximum theoretical speed or output, we arrive at the minimum order time and highest productivity level; in this ideal world, there would be no defects. The maximum average rate from the utopian state can be compared with the actual average rate, and the minimum order time can be compared with the actual order time.

While this scenario may appear hypothetical, we have constructed well over two hundred such profiles in diverse industries. These were organizations with respectable rates against standards, many in the high-90 percent of standard. They were surprised to see that on average they were getting 40 percent of the possible output, instead of the 90+ percent of standard. This realization created a paradigm shift. It also focused improvement efforts on the specific areas of greatest opportunity for their particular processes. This focus on the key losses (setup, inertial, speed, downtime, and quality losses) then drove improvement efforts that brought their profiles closer to the utopian condition.

While we have primarily related the process productivity profile to the manufacturing sector, profiling of the same five losses is equally applicable to the service sector. As an illustration that most readers will relate to, let's look at the process of preparing an expense account. First we have to get ready—get out the necessary forms and receipts. The time above the minimum is setup or changeover losses, as we are changing from one task to the current task. Having gotten everything ready, we typically see inertial losses as we start slowly and build our speed. Even though we may never get to maximum speed due to any number of factors, while at speed we are often interrupted, thus creating downtime losses. To illustrate how common it is to see inertial losses as we restart after a downtime, consider the following. Suppose you are at your desk, working away in this case on your expense account. The phone rings, and it is a wrong number. You hang up, and as you go back to your expense account, what do you say to yourself? (See the most common answer at the end of this chapter.) Your speed builds again until the expense account is complete. Notice that you are most error-prone during the setup, inertial loss, and downtime periods.

Finally, reviewing Exhibit 6.7, we can see the effect on costs and delivery from both reducing the non-value-adding steps and improving the value-adding steps with the system productivity profile. Notice that the costs are lowered, quality is improved, and cycle time is shortened, thus making the enterprise leaner and more attractive to customers.

CONTEMPORARY BUSINESS MODEL

The company in our case story is a producer of aluminum foil for industrial products and the packaging industry. It is a multimillion-dollar producer of aluminum for heat exchangers, automotive body side molding, pharmaceutical closures, food containers, and industrial applications.

Much of the aluminum foil produced is run through a coater that puts a protective and/or decorative coating on the aluminum sheet and foil. The coater is about 150 feet long and two stories high. Coils of aluminum sheet or foil—up to four feet in diameter and six feet wide and weighing as much as eight thousand pounds—are fed into the coater from an un-

EXHIBIT 6.7   Value Adding versus Non–Value Adding

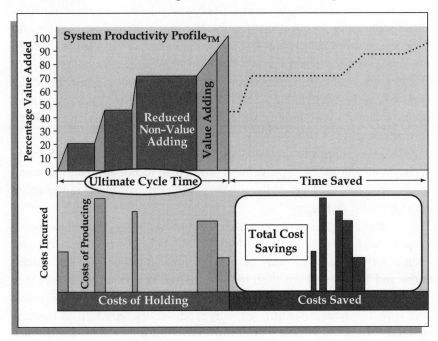

wind stand. These coils are washed clean of rolling lubricants in a wash station, printed or coated by a direct gravure process, and heated to set and cure the coatings in a flotation oven. Then the coated material is wound upon spools at the output end of the machine.

When another plant within the system permanently shut down its coater due to age and needed maintenance, the volume shifted to the subject plant. With this change in manufacturing capacity and a strong metal sales market, there was pressure to generate more quality throughput from the coater, and to do so quickly. Extrapolating the expected needs and opportunities, a productivity improvement project was established with a goal of a 25 percent increase in safely produced, quality-coated product. The emphasis on safety and quality was intentional, as *there was to be no compromise in either safety or quality.* One of the authors, Bill Houser, had just successfully completed helping the plant become certified to the international quality standard ISO 9000 and the automotive quality standard QS-9000, and he was asked to act as a consultant for this project.

This desired 25 percent targeted increase in productivity was very aggressive because the coater was already staffed by four crews continuously operating twenty-four hours per day (including breaks and lunches), seven days per week. Obviously, increasing the hours through additional shifts or overtime was not an option. To put the magnitude of the 25 percent goal in perspective, with official statistics reporting at the time that in the United States, annual productivity growth was averaging about 1 percent, we needed twenty-five years of productivity gains in a few months.

Because timing was an issue and capital was limited, they decided to focus on methodology improvement rather than technology improvement to reach the goal. They believed that the gains could be made more quickly and with less cost.

Houser recognized that for many processes, operating *methodology* has not kept pace with the *technology* that has been provided. In other words, technologically it may be possible for many processes to produce more and better products than they are currently providing. In fact, it is very common for equipment to have been purchased with the expectation that it will provide quantum leaps in productivity only to find that the gains are marginal at best. These unfulfilled promises of higher quality and productivity often cause those providing the capital to doubt the wisdom of their investments in improved equipment. In many such cases, the issue is not one of flawed technology, but rather that the methods to operate these processes have not been as refined as the technology they serve. To get the most from today's processes, it is necessary to study and improve the *methodology* by which the processes are operated. This was the approach chosen to increase the coater productivity.

Focusing on the Opportunity

In making throughput improvements, they needed to identify the specific priority areas of opportunity for improvement, and then exploit the prioritized areas to their full potential for added production. The productivity profile was used as both a conceptual and diagnostic visual model to focus on the opportunity for additional coater throughput and to develop priority areas for improvement. Using available production data and observations, Houser and the senior coater engineer, Al Kennedy, quickly constructed a productivity profile for the coater, and they carefully examined the five categories of potential production losses to determine the prioritized areas for improvement. The productivity profile revealed the losses were in the following priority order:

1. *Downtime losses* of all types were the largest of the five losses. They became the priority focus for reduction, as the production data showed a 75 percent reduction would result in exceeding the goal of a 25 percent increase in throughput.

2. *Changeover losses* associated with going from one coated item to another were second-largest. Although a priority area for improvement, the production data indicated that reducing the changeover losses by 75 percent would make less than a 10 percent difference in the overall productivity.

3. *Speed losses* from running below machine/coating potential were only significant if new coatings could be developed that allowed running quality production at higher speeds. This was the third priority as developing new coatings and coating practices was determined to be a longer-range objective.

4. *Quality/waste losses*, though significant, were associated primarily with issues involving the prior three primary losses. These losses would decrease as the downtime, changeover, and speed losses were reduced.

5. *Inertial losses* were practically nonexistent, so no potential gain was available in this category.

Since the downtime losses represented the majority of all losses, they were further analyzed. This effort resulted in the recognition that the downtime losses fell into two categories: random machine downtimes and coil changes. The random machine downtimes, the smaller of the two categories, consisted of such things as incinerator problems, metal defects, and oven shutdowns. The larger downtime loss was associated with the periodic coil changes—in other words, loading new material onto the coater, removing the coated material, and testing the product. The production data showed that the coil change time represented over 40 percent of the total production losses; therefore, coil change became the highest priority for improvement.

Improving Coil Changes

The classical definition for changeovers is the time and actions it takes to go from producing one product to producing the next product. Coater coil changes do not fit this definition because they do not involve going from producing one product to another—the same product is being produced both before and after the coil change. This is exactly the reason that those with dedicated equipment (dedicated to producing a single product) often do not believe they have changeovers.

The production data showed that a coil change required an average of 53 minutes (0.9 hours), and there was an average of 4.6 coil changes per day. This means that more than four hours (0.9 hours × 4.6 coil changes/day = 4.14 hours) per day of the twenty-four hours available were consumed in routine coil changes. If the coil change could be reduced to fifteen minutes, the productive time would be increased by more than three hours per day, with a more than 20 percent improvement in total productivity. Therefore, a coil change target of fifteen minutes was established.

Houser and Kennedy made a process map of the coil change, which entailed determining all the steps necessary to install a new coil of aluminum on the coater. To do so, they videotaped coil changes and flowcharted the process. A great deal of care was taken to involve the coater crews in the process from start to finish, and all four crews were videotaped. The crews appreciated the opportunity to participate and showcase their talents.

Two people comprised each coater crew—one at the operating or unwind end and one at the output or rewind end of the machine. At the beginning of each coil change, the coater is shut down, and one of the crew goes to each end. As the empty mill sleeve is removed from the unwind end and a full coil of uncoated aluminum is moved into position, the full coil of coated material is *typically* removed from the rewind end. (We say "typically" because a lot of variation in the coil change process was noted among the four crews.)

A splice is then made by taping the end of the last run to the beginning of the coil of uncoated material brought into position at the unwind end. Because the tape could stand no more than 200 degrees Fahrenheit and the coater oven runs at temperatures up to 600 degrees, there was a wait until the oven dropped below 200 degrees before the splice could be run through. After the splice was run through, the coater oven could be brought back up to operating temperatures and the coating run started.

When coated material was through the machine, it would be stopped and a sample would be cut from the rewind end and taken into the lab for testing.

A number of steps were taken to improve the basic process and ensure consistency across the crews. By locating a splicing tape that would withstand 400 degrees, the wait for the furnace to cool down to 200 degrees and heat back up again could be eliminated. Unfortunately, the tape did not have the tensile strength of the tape it replaced. The lower strength and the existing practice resulted in frequent sheet breaks. There were successes, but the failures were dramatic, with aluminum shooting out of both ends of the coater when a splice broke. This outcome caused a great deal of frustration and some lost time, but a lot of learning also resulted from the failures. With each coil change videotaped, the splice-running technique was diagnosed and evolved until the furnaces could run reliably at operating temperatures. The end results of the study were consistency in how coils were changed; energy saved by maintaining temperatures in the oven; quicker, better, and more reliable lab tests; and coil change times under the fifteen-minute goal. The coater productivity was up over 25 percent in about two months.

SUMMARY

Dieters realize they must find and use the most effective measurements. Doing so leads to greater insight and eventually breakthroughs in the diet. Firms using the Wall Street Diet similarly will find insights and breakthroughs using the tools described in this chapter. "Good enough" usually isn't.

The Wall Street Diet introduces tools that will help the firm achieve a healthier end state. The horn of uncertainty addresses inaccurate forecasting. Reducing cycle times and uncertainty will demonstrably improve forecasting and directly leads to reduced costs and better information utilization.

As the Wall Street Diet is implemented, there must be a means of determining the need for the effort, or participants lose interest and resist the discipline. We have found no better tool than the productivity profile to identify the current conditions, generally to the chagrin of people responsible for a process after numerous improvement efforts have been completed. The proofing technique is easily applied to any process and compares theoretical utopian conditions against current performance, in a way that pinpoints the areas of value-adding and non-value-adding effort, thereby indicating the greatest impact and opportunity for improvement.

In numerous instances, we have been able to document that some important processes are operating as low as 10 to 20 percent of capacity. By bringing a process closer to optimized conditions, with the help of the operators and crews, and then using the higher performance as a target for similar operations, the total effectiveness of a business is improved. As the technique is extended to supply chain partners, the network benefits and distinguishes itself in the eyes of the customers.

CHECKLIST FOR SENIOR MANAGEMENT

- ☐ Do not be lulled into complacency when your reports show results are acceptable. The right tools and measures might yield additional ways to increase your profits dramatically.
- ☐ Support innovative approaches. If they do not work, they will lead to approaches that will.
- ☐ Insist that each direct report bring to you one area where the profiling tool will be applied.

CHECKLIST FOR FUNCTIONAL MANAGERS AND DIET CHAMPIONS

- ☐ Build a new tool kit. Include process maps, the productivity profile, and other innovations to discover hidden profits.
- ☐ Select an area that is particularly impacted by poor forecasts. Establish a team to use the horn of uncertainty and other techniques described in this chapter to reduce the uncertainty and the cycle time involved.
- ☐ Search for and eliminate non-value-adding steps. They began as someone's good idea, but now they add costs, not value.
- ☐ Set up a pilot project, using the profiling tool, to determine areas where especially low utilization and productivity are present.

Answer to the question: Over 90 percent of those responding to the question "What do you say to yourself when you restart a process after being interrupted is?" said, "Now, where was I?" or some variation thereof.

Don't Do It Yourself—Outsource to Change Your Lifestyle

Part of the dieting process is intensely personal. An individual's decision to change lifestyle leads to hundreds of smaller decisions to keep on the diet. But there is a far more public part of the process that involves other people.

For example, as the dieter changes years of bad habits, people notice. The body slims, clothes fit better, and the individual radiates a new health. When a business starts to shed its years of bad habits, people will also notice. They may even show their appreciation by buying stock.

In addition, the dieter must also bring other people into the process. Family and friends provide support. Specialists with skills and expertise that the dieter simply does not have may be necessary if the dieter has reached a plateau: A nutritionist may help improve eating habits and recommend supplements; a doctor may be required for medical attention, especially if there is a crisis; a personal trainer may provide the right kind of exercise that the dieter may otherwise discover only by trial and error. In short, to succeed in changing a lifestyle, the dieter must go beyond the do-it-yourself phase to break new ground and achieve lasting success.

The business must also take a cold, hard look at the do-it-yourself approach and ask whether a better way is possible. The Wall Street Diet adopts the approach that selective outsourcing of processes and operations to key strategic partners is the way to break new ground in finding process improvements.

This chapter explores the hardest part of the Wall Street Diet, as we consider trimming parts of the organization's infrastructure and carefully selecting and turning process steps over to more capable business partners within the value-managed enterprise. The firm has already developed expertise in three other components of the diet—advanced supply chain management, lean management, and quality management. After extensive work, some areas within the firm probably have not matured and adapted as well as the others.

We go now in search of other reasons for high cholesterol and clogged arteries in a business, as we seek out where the firm has become bloated or not as trim as a potential supplier. As we do, don't be surprised if a portion of the reasons for excess costs are rooted in practices and beliefs relating to how to work with willing supply chain partners. We refer here to the general lack of trust companies place in even the most important and long-standing suppliers—from letting them handle a larger portion of raw material needs, components, or subassemblies to fully outsourcing the actual manufacturing process.

In essence, the selective outsourcing ingredient in the diet calls for a careful examination of the dieter's lifestyle to determine areas of weakness or simply less-than-adequate approaches. Remember, the successful diet is not just about losing weight. It's a matter of adopting a different, healthy lifestyle.

Outsourcing may fundamentally alter the firm's identity. As in advanced supply chain management, tremendous advantages can be gained by transferring key processes and operations to trusted network allies. If an external source can perform the same function or process step more effectively than it can be done internally, the firm can potentially move away from do-it-yourself to another level of business improvement and success.

As a new way of working for most people, outsourcing is the area where we will uncover profound resistance to the diet regimen. Understanding and coping with this resistance begins with consideration of the normal reluctance to treat key suppliers as strategic partners as well as the difficulty with shutting down internal processing so that an outsider can do the work. Old habits are detrimental to the new lifestyle. Success in the diet depends on eliminating these bad habits—even if they are the "sacred cow" habits of an organization's history.

OPPORTUNITIES AND DIFFICULTIES

The search for trimming business costs by having others perform necessary processes more effectively can be as simple as contracting with another firm to do the billing or handle the payrolls, typical areas given over to outsourcing. These outsourcing arrangements typically focus on administrative or support areas. They do not threaten a firm's identity.

Perhaps an entire function can be placed in the hands of more capable processors, such as data processing. This may seem like heresy, but it can prove to be a powerful strategy.

Dynegy Inc., a $6 billion, Houston-based energy company, found this to be the case regarding its information technology (IT) function. The firm was dragged into the debacle at neighbor Enron and was under great scrutiny, including its accounting methods. Dynegy had an IT group that was considerably larger than what was needed for its operations after a market-forced downsizing. According to senior vice president and CIO Steve Moffitt, "We were stuck with a technology infrastructure built to support a $40 billion company, and that's not where Dynegy was anymore." After careful consideration, the company made the decision to outsource IT to another specialist firm. That move not only saved money but contributed to the resolution of most of the firm's legal troubles and reduced debt by two-thirds (McDougall 2004: 45). Few firms would take the dramatic step of outsourcing such a vital function, but it was essential for Dynegy to do so. This move was far bolder than outsourcing billing, for example, but, again, it does not threaten the identity of the firm.

When it comes to outsourcing a process step within the manufacturing arena, other circumstances are encountered, and much greater resistance can be expected. Here, the firm's traditional identity may in fact be threatened. Two sides quickly form when outsourcing is considered. Proponents point to internal weaknesses and suggest more capable external sources can provide the same quality at lower costs. Opponents decry the potential of such sources and lobby to keep all processing within the four walls of the business.

In this area, simply sourcing materials and parts to a supplier can introduce problems, particularly where there is a decided lack of trust between the parties. Often the buyer is characterized as trying to dominate the relationship. The supplier then views the buyer with suspicion or believes the buyer is using a heavy-handed approach to negotiations. In such a charged atmosphere, the supplier is going to be very careful in making offerings and will be wary in its pricing.

Within certain industries, this adversarial relation is considered sacrosanct. Few within the buying firm question the relationship, because "It's always been this way." The suppliers are forced into a defensive position, and they hardly look like strategic allies when their first priority is to protect themselves from a predatory buyer.

To illustrate this type of situation, consider a study by automotive researcher John Henke Jr. Focusing on long-standing business practices, he compared the potential excess costs of the so-called Big Three car manufacturers and Japanese competitors.

Henke concludes that "supplying a component to the Big Three automakers costs 8 percent more on average than supplying a similar part to Toyota Motor or Honda Motor companies, even when the parts came from the same supplier" (Chappell 2004). His report shows that parts makers to the automotive industry believe bad relations with suppliers are hurting those buyers. Henke blames the higher costs to the Big Three on these factors:

- Higher administrative costs to meet quality and compliance standards
- Staff hours tied up in price wrangling
- Time spent resolving problems
- Other costs associated with servicing the contract throughout a vehicle program

These are real costs in the system that must be absorbed. They are not inflated prices just to increase the price. It is possible to drive these costs out of the system.

Henke's point revolves around the idea that suppliers will generally bring greater offerings, more innovative ideas and features, to buyers willing to work in a more collaborative environment than to those accustomed to heavy-handed negotiations.

The Big Three deny an 8 percent advantage can exist. It does. A second study, this one by Liker and Choi (2004) in the *Harvard Business Review*, echoes Henke's comments. Liker and Choi analyzed how Honda and Toyota build supplier relationships compared to the Big Three. According to these researchers, the "Two Japanese automakers have had stunning success building relationships with North American suppliers—often the same companies that have had contentious dealings with Detroit's Big Three" (104). Throughout a lengthy and detailed analysis, these authors describe how Honda and Toyota made it their business to apply lean concepts coupled with a supplier relationship management (SRM) strategy that focused on developing key suppliers rather than forcing them into making price concessions.

The Wall Street Diet must be carefully applied, and it is here that the larger picture is crucial. There is absolutely no sense in applying any of the three disciplines we have considered so far to a fundamentally flawed process. Why make a bad process more efficient?

We must mention another fundamental concern: No firm wants to admit that it is not the best at what is has been chartered to do in virtually all parts of the business. The Wall Street Diet stresses the controversial point that business partnering with carefully selected suppliers is the lifeblood of a successful supply chain. We have just shown that this is especially true when discussing how a firm selects its sourcing base or the results of negotiating what should be industry-best pricing. Few firms want to acknowledge that they have not extracted every ounce of savings possible from their supply base, or that they have overlooked added values that could be presented by those suppliers. Our experiences indicate that the purchasing community in general thrives on the belief that the best possible deal has been made on all key sourcing categories.

But the facts overwhelmingly speak to segments of every business we have studied that have not kept up to contemporary standards. We find few companies that do not have at least one area that should be put on a diet or considered for outsourcing. Firms that are not using the Wall Street Diet would much rather do things for themselves, even with great pride. This do-it-yourself attitude gets in the way of business realities.

In a personal incident, one of the authors was working with a well-branded firm making weed control and lawn grooming equipment as well as a long line of motorized hand tools. During a casual plant site inspection, a huge opportunity was exposed.

As part of the visit, the plant manager pointed out to the author how the firm was winding its own fractional horsepower motors. A large area of floor space was dedicated to this operation, and the equipment being used was all pre-1960s. The author asked for figures on total delivered costs for motors ranging from one-eighth to one horsepower. The plant manager proudly provided metrics, along with charts showing eight consecutive quarters of productivity improvement. After a few telephone calls and e-mails, it was substantiated that costs across the line of motors could be reduced by 20 to 25 percent by sourcing from foreign suppliers, which would be using machines with nameplate dates that all started with 1990 and later. The plant manager refused to believe what he was hearing but did agree to a pilot test to compare costs and quality. The firm subsequently quietly outsourced its motor needs to better-able suppliers.

OUTSOURCING IS A BITTER PILL—BUT POWERFUL MEDICINE—FOR MANY FIRMS

A manufacturing organization regularly makes decisions about the acquisition of parts, supplies, or materials that go directly into the core products and the production of subassemblies that result in finished goods. Outsourcing here can be the most obvious but most difficult-to-accept part of the business to consider, for two reasons: the need to get supplies that cannot be manufactured at competitive costs from reliable sources, and the need to do in-house manufacturing at, or near, industry-best levels of performance.

Selective outsourcing begins with having trusting and mutually beneficial relationships with the strategic suppliers.

When a company needs supplies from external sources, purchasing, procurement, and sourcing have been synonymous with negotiating to get the lowest possible costs. The evidence demonstrates that strict adherence to the use of tough leverage leads to diminishing returns. The traditional concept has not been viable in the long term. We have seen greater value for both parties introduced through analytics and changes aimed at getting to the best possible processing for both the firm and the external source.

Jack Welch, former chairman of General Electric Corporation, told the managers at GE to either be number one or number two in an industry or get out of that business. It took very forceful senior leadership to enact the intended principles, but the results are the making of business history. The ideas inherent in Welch's dramatic moves have been adopted in supply chain thinking.

What this view means today is that a firm should periodically analyze the process steps in its end-to-end supply chain and match performance against reliable benchmarks. It should be best or a close second-best at each step. If not, these steps should be turned over to a more capable business partner. Therein lies the essence of selective outsourcing—business decisions aimed at keeping the firm as trim and responsive as possible.

This leadership orientation requires elevating the role of the buyers to strategic partners. They become skilled analysts and business drivers, bringing carefully selected suppliers inside the firm, at high levels, to have a direct impact on which process steps should be done internally and which are better placed in the hands of an external source. Industry leaders realize this is done without compromising the viability of the business.

In the realm of advanced supply chain management, those responsible for the sourcing function work with a handful of key suppliers to build competitive advantages for the business. Within such an environment, these key sourcing officials work with the most strategic suppliers through a new form of SRM. A better relationship for buyer and seller is possible if rewards are shared. The heart of this new approach is the idea that many suppliers are better able to add value by doing more with the materials and parts supplied than the customer. The parties determine jointly where the actual point of handoff should occur.

A major supplier of aerospace equipment to the military provides a dramatic example. This firm was diligently developing the latest in such equipment, particularly a lighter, faster, and more maneuverable airplane to carry troops into battle and function as a sophisticated fighting machine. There was strong demand for this equipment from several branches of the military. Funds were limited, and the time frame to meet desired delivery schedules was tight.

One of the authors facilitated a partnering diagnostic lab (detailed in the appendix). Several large suppliers, one of which was a competitor, were invited to dissect the process map for the new aircraft. The lab established the fact that assembly time could be substantially reduced if larger subassemblies were made by the suppliers rather than the manufacturer. Essentially, the diagnostic revealed that the manufacturer was best at final assembly and testing, but not at preparing some of the subparts. Several component parts were already being created by suppliers that could accommodate additional work, eliminating the need to do the work at the manufacturing site. The savings per unit were also important when decisions were made on which parts would be made externally (including some by the competitor) and which would be kept in-house.

In his book *Good to Great*, Jim Collins (2001) makes a similar point. As Collins describes firms that have exceeded others in an industry and the market in general, he cites the case of Kimberly-Clark, a venerable and respected paper company. Demonstrating the power of outsourcing, the CEO decided to take a bold move. He sold the paper mills. In addition, he proceeded to buy the products needed for the business from the new mill owners at prices lower than previous manufactured costs. The proceeds from the sale of assets were used to enhance the already-strong Kleenex brand image, while moving the branding into other products—toilet tissues and disposable diapers. In essence, he had carefully outsourced some very core operations to others more capable of operating those assets. By buying back the same products at lower costs, he took advantage of core competencies possessed outside his organization.

In another example, one of the authors was working with one of North America's largest private-label beverage bottlers. This firm was struggling against the established soft drink bottlers, such as Coca-Cola, PepsiCo, and Dr Pepper–Seven-Up. The company also operated its own blending and bottling operations. It conducted an in-depth analysis to determine whether it should continue to operate its bottling plants or subcontract that function to more capable suppliers. The analysis revealed that all but two of the operations were considerably higher in total delivered cost than what could be achieved with other sources, including some firms doing bottling for Coke and Pepsi. The company eventually moved its manufacturing to the contract bottlers (reducing costs by as much as 25 percent) and concentrated on developing more private-label customers (which increased by more than 10 percent).

Outsourcing must be thoroughly reviewed, critiqued, and tested, and it generally works best with a carefully chosen pilot to verify the expected results.

Just as a dieter discovers that greater progress can be made by working with others, these firms learned that a do-it-yourself attitude was eroding profits, slowing deliveries, and turning out less than world-class products.

A New View of Supplier Relationship Management

Simply stated, the Wall Street Diet calls for harmonizing what suppliers can provide through strategic sourcing to end-user applications. It includes working with key suppliers to determine whether and when externally sourced materials, parts, or supplies can offset higher costs of manufacture or assembly. Most important, the diet calls for working across businesses to find the information and systems that will enhance performance for all supply chain partners. Successful SRM aligns, coordinates, and integrates all of these activities into an efficient, seamless process. It embraces and links the different partners with their data throughout the value chain.

Returning briefly to the automotive industry for yet another example, Liker and Choi have spent years studying the difference between Honda and Toyota and the Big Three Detroit manufacturers. The former are substantially ahead of the latter in terms of prices paid for parts and introduction of innovative design and developments. Toyota and Honda do not go to third world areas for lower prices, for example, but rely more on long-term suppliers to work closely with their engineers to find cost-saving advantages and consumer-friendly features.

Working relationships with suppliers are close partnerships under the Japanese system and arm's-length, bitterly fought conditions under the U.S. system. When discussing how the two Japanese firms found success making cars at U.S. plants, these analysts note, "Toyota and Honda have managed to replicate in an alien Western culture the same kind of supplier webs they built in Japan. Consequently, they enjoy the best supplier relations in the U.S. automobile industry, have the fastest product development processes, and reduce costs and improve quality year after year" (Liker and Choi 2004: 106).

When the Japanese carmakers established manufacturing facilities in the United States, they brought their Taiichi Ohno– (creator of the Toyota production system) inspired lean concepts with them, encouraging keiretsu-like joint ventures with American suppliers and bringing down the cost of building Camry and Accord models by 25 percent during the 1990s. As an example of how the firms approach selective outsourcing, Toyota divides car components into two categories: those that vendors can design and those that must be developed internally. When the firm decided to build cars in Kentucky, it selected Johnson Controls to supply the seats. The story about that situation speaks volumes in terms of the different approaches taken by the rival companies:

Johnson Controls wanted to expand its nearby facility, but Toyota stipulated that it shouldn't, partly because an expansion would require a large investment

and eat into the supplier's profits. Instead, the Japanese manufacturer chal-
lenged Johnson Controls to make more seats in an existing building. That
seemed impossible at first, but with the help of Toyota's lean manufacturing
experts, the supplier restructured its shop floor, slashed inventories, and was
able to make seats for Toyota in the existing space. (Liker and Choi 2004: 110)

Finding business partners with better qualifications to complete those
process steps and improve overall effectiveness is the new sourcing quest.
These suppliers may be unknown to those responsible for the internal
process steps. We stress this concept as part of the Wall Street Diet in spite
of the fact that most outsourcing fails to receive high satisfaction ratings,
especially among those with vested interests at stake. Our experience indicates the failure rate is more a factor of poor initial planning and continued cultural resistance.

BALANCING COST WITH PERFORMANCE

Cost discussions will always be part of the sourcing process, even as
greater collaboration is considered. The Wall Street Diet broadens that discussion by asking where those costs should reside in a supply chain. Costs
should be viewed within the context of operations, as part of an overall
evaluation of asset utilization. As an element of the Wall Street Diet, asset
utilization asks which party should own or operate the assets, for greatest
value to the network.

Our most successful efforts occur when we are able to get a few members of an extended enterprise to sit down and consider the basic features
of a network. By moving to more complex descriptions, analyzing the important process flows, and giving frank consideration to best possible
practices across the end-to-end processing, we invariably find ways to enhance asset ownership and asset utilization. Putting the right process
steps in the hands of the most capable business constituent is the intention, and overlooked possibilities always turn up in the diagnostic.

The typical result of such diagnostics is a movement up the maturity
scale, as shown in Exhibit 7.1, where we see the supplier relationship and
the role of the strategic buyer advance from the traditional negotiation
view to a full alliance, in which key suppliers have an active part in helping the firm develop its strategy and execute its business plans. The
process will invariably progress to the second stage, where the full vol-

EXHIBIT 7.1 Emerging Sourcing Strategies

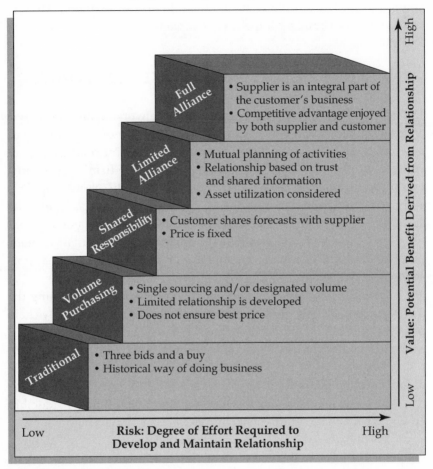

ume of the business is leveraged, often to single sources, to achieve better pricing. In the third stage, the negotiating parties begin to realize that there is mutual value in a less confrontational approach, and they begin to work together. The focus will often be on better forecasting and planning to find savings for both firms. In the fourth stage, a limited alliance is formed with a very select group of suppliers, and the buying firm begins building a model more in keeping with the Wall Street Diet. Now the two parties are studying the flowchart to find savings for both companies. As illustrated, the highest level, where alliances blossom, can result in the greatest potential value. It is here that a few businesses have overcome the do-it-yourself attitude and the lack of trust of suppliers. They are hard at work using key suppliers as an integral part of the organization to work together to build a competitive advantage.

NETWORK SOLUTIONS BECOME THE TARGET

The Wall Street Diet moves a company and its network to this higher level of business maturity, as described in Exhibit 7.2. The move is from a focus on transactions, cost control, and efficiency to a drive for productivity, involving suppliers in planning and execution of the firm's processing. Eventually, higher levels are reached, where the carefully selected suppliers and outsourced organizations have gained trust and are codeveloping and using supply chain systems. In the highest level, the value network has been established, and new benefits are being found for all partners, especially through advanced communication technologies and real-time sharing of knowledge.

Exhibit 7.2 describes the approach we recommend. Preceding the transformation phases, the firm outlines a description of the supply chain processing. Data should be collected to verify actual current costs and reliable external benchmarks for comparison. A core team should be appointed to develop a risk-and-reward chart and create a preliminary vision and strategy for the careful selective outsourcing to follow. During this phase, the firm constructs a case for action and aligns leadership around what will be controversial moves.

In the first phase of the model, the team makes its initial pass at selecting possible opportunities, areas that jump out from the process map as being candidates. Partnering diagnostic laboratories (PDLs) are especially beneficial at uncovering possibilities (see the appendix). These labs involve a one-day preparation meeting with the sponsoring firm and one or two selected suppliers and a two-day intensive diagnostic to generate a specific list of potential improvement areas.

In the second phase, the team takes care to establish the current state—a frank and detailed view of what is happening in the chosen process. Now team members are assigned to gather internal and industry data, relying often on suppliers to provide hard-to-get information. The focus must be on the total costs involved.

In the third phase, attention turns to developing the sourcing or selective outsourcing strategies. Now the team, with the help of a few suppliers,

EXHIBIT 7.2 Selective Outsourcing Methodology

Phase 0: Enterprise Diagnostic and Strategy	**Phase 1:** Selected Opportunities	**Phase 2:** Establish Current State	**Phase 3:** Develop Sourcing Strategies	**Phase 4:** Negotiate and Contract	**Phase 5:** Operate and Maintain
• Develop analysis straw man • Develop data collection strategy • Collect and analyze data: procurement category map, opportunity matrix • Develop risk/reward analysis • Create enterprise vision and strategy • Build case for action • Begin leadership alignment	• Use partnering diagnostic laboratory to select process steps and analyze opportunities • Identify and recruit participants • Orient team and train participants • Develop team charter and work plans	• Collect internal company data • Collect external industry data • Map current processes • Prepare request for information (RFI) • Develop total cost of ownership (TCO) model • Use PDL to refine opportunities	• Conduct best practices research • Analyze internal and external data • Redesign processes • Develop strategies • Develop prioritized action plans and secure buy-in • Build action matrix	• Establish partnering requirements • Assemble buyer's strategic supplier list, actions, deliverables • Involve key suppliers in internal strategy and business plans • Issue contracts for processing • Evaluate performance • Communicate selections and results to key stakeholders	• Develop supplier/buyer "alliance" plan • Execute plan • Conduct scorecard review sessions • Develop relationship • Relaunch team (if necessary)

conducts best-practice research—inside the industry and across other industries. High-cost or low-efficiency processes become clear candidates for redesign or are placed in the hands of another organization. Pilot tests may be required to verify the potential improvements, but order-of-magnitude figures relating to costs and benefits must appear at this stage. Using a PDL, the team usually comes up with a prioritized list of improvement opportunities, complete with action plans for testing. In any event, an action matrix including priority rating and time frame to execute should be created to help gain alignment and to secure buy-in to at least the pilot testing.

In the fourth phase, the actual negotiation and contracting occur, but with much greater emphasis on the collaborative aspects and drive for mutual benefits than the traditional heavy leveraging. Partnering requirements are established for both parties. The buyer's strategic supplier list is discussed with an eye to determining how more value can be provided, including assumption of some of the manufacturing responsibility. Key suppliers now become involved in helping with the internal strategy and business plans. Contracts are issued for the redesigned processing, with accepted performance evaluations. Results are, of course, communicated to the key stakeholders, especially regarding test or performance measures that verify the intended improvements.

Finally, in the fifth phase, the partners work on operating the redesigned systems and maintaining the values added. That means the process is continuous. Supplier-buyer alliance plans replace traditional contracts. Execution of the plan is tracked and publicized. A scorecard is maintained to validate the improvements and to serve as a proof of concept. Efforts are constant to enhance the new relationship and extend it to other process steps.

CONTEMPORARY BUSINESS MODEL

One of the leading outsourcers of all time offers plentiful examples of the positive aspects of this approach. Dell Computer has developed an international reputation for its direct-sales model. Dell's model assumes all parts should be outsourced and brought in just-in-time to make customized final assemblies for each specific customer. What is less known about the model is the manner in which Dell approaches its global supplier relationships and manages its SRM system.

Like other firms concentrating on operational excellence, Dell focuses on increasing sales revenues and eliminating wastes. Early in its quest to outsource on a global basis, Dell tried to move too quickly with supplier development. It underestimated the necessary training these new sources would need and did not properly match the inflows with the segmentation demanded by its business model.

As Dell progressed with its outsourcing strategy, it developed stronger and closer relationships to ensure the viability of its far-flung supply base. One example of the mutual values to be derived from such an orientation is provided by analysts Fugate and Mentzer (2004):

> *Dell leverages its partners by linking suppliers' planning and execution activities with Dell's systems. The suppliers are expected to share information such as capacity outlooks and new technology drivers. In return, Dell provides direct signals of customer demand to suppliers and shares current and projected market shifts and sourcing strategies. At the same time, the company's extranet—its dedicated Internet link with outside partners—enhances collaboration on, and commitment to, forecasts. This visibility up and down the supply chain allows Dell to manage demand in real time.* (23)

This feature also enables the suppliers to match supply with demand in a manner almost unequaled in the high-technology industry.

SUMMARY

This chapter covers the most difficult part of the Wall Street Diet, as we encourage a firm to assess its weight and responsiveness and loosen its do-it-yourself attitude. What could be done better by someone else? A close look will reveal opportunities within a supply chain. We strongly encourage the would-be dieter to consider a major shift in orientation around how to acquire materials, supplies, parts, and services as well as whether or not the firm is the most capable business partner to perform all of the processes kept in-house. As the evaluation is made, the role of those responsible for strategic sourcing and supplier relationship management must move to a higher level—from fierce negotiator to key strategist.

We have supplied a number of examples of how and where this new orientation works. What is required is a transformation to the culture of the business from a confrontational approach to sourcing and supplier involvement in manufacturing, to a more collaborative style that embodies the lean concepts and advanced supply chain management techniques that are a part of the Wall Street Diet.

CHECKLIST FOR SENIOR MANAGEMENT

☐ Prepare to eliminate sacred cows.

☐ Focus on the network's capacity—not the firm's capacity—to produce the best product at the most acceptable costs.

☐ Enforce the idea that suppliers are not the enemy. They could be your strongest allies.

☐ Recognize that your firm may not be the best in every area, and challenge the business and functional leaders to develop examples of situations where their units may not be best or second-best at a specific process.

CHECKLIST FOR FUNCTIONAL MANAGERS AND DIET CHAMPIONS

☐ Arrange a partnering diagnostic lab with a few trusted external advisers, particularly a key supplier. Sit down with the process map, and identify process steps that are not up to industry-best standards or highly efficient.

☐ Use the PDL to validate the potential improvements.

☐ Use external data and benchmarking information available in most industries or through qualified experts to establish the gap in performance. For the identified area, set up a pilot to test an external source for, say, ninety days.

☐ Go online and solicit bids for the processing, and compare prices with internal costs. Try auctions to see whether fabricated parts can be bought for less than what they can be produced internally.

☐ If you persist in your desire to keep the processing inside the business, at least establish some external standards that are meaningful, and challenge the internal group to match those standards within, say, six months.

ADOPT A NEW LIFESTYLE—FOCUS ON CUSTOMER SATISFACTION

At this point, our dieter has achieved several measures of success. It's time to pause and remember what the goal was at the beginning of the diet.

For some, the issue was clearly health. A life-threatening condition demanded immediate and permanent changes to the dieter's lifestyle. Bad habits were literally killing the individual. Using all the tools available, the dieter has changed and now looks forward to a more normal life. Life is the reward.

For others, a diet leads to a lifestyle change with more freedom. The individual can do more things with added energy and mobility. Movement is much easier.

The successful dieter is now free to choose from a wider selection of clothing. It's not just a new wardrobe. The successful dieter can choose among fashions, stores, and price ranges.

The dieter may have increased self-esteem added to the new image. Families, friends, and colleagues notice and compliment the dieter. There may be reward or incentives earned for reaching specific levels.

All such positive outcomes are terrific, but the key to remember is that this healthier lifestyle must also be maintained. It can be easy to slip back into old habits, but the successful dieter who has learned that "nothing tastes as good as fit feels" has no desire to return to the old ways.

To continue enjoying success, the dieter wants to have access to the latest knowledge on things behind the diet or supporting the new lifestyle. Consider, for example, all of the products and news items that showed up following the low-carb diet craze.

A firm that has come this far in the Wall Street Diet has also reached new levels of achievement and has become a streamlined, more effective enterprise that now can turn its attention more acutely to revenue. All along, a focus has been on the customer. Now is the time to take advantage of this attention and capitalize on the gains from the diet.

Application of technology becomes necessary at this phase. The firm that applies the Wall Street Diet wants to be sure that knowledge critical for driving further gains is easily accessed on a real-time basis. That means customer intelligence must be used to keep up-to-date and sharing of vital data must continue, or the gains will be lost.

Through the Wall Street Diet, firms achieve cost improvements that bring some of the five to eight points of potential new profit to the bottom line. They should also see benefits to planning, order management and processing, order-to-cash cycle times, just-in-time deliveries, and inventory management as the firm moves into the advanced levels of supply chain management and healthier business conditions. With these diet gains in place, the sharper focus will be on establishing greater customer satisfaction, so achievements should also be made to on-time deliveries, fill rates, returns, and other measures important to the customer.

The hard work will have a payoff in more appreciation by important customers, which now see a leaner and more responsive company and supporting enterprise partners. These customers expect the new body to be more agile, quicker in response time, less costly to deal with, and so forth. The reward to the firm will be additional revenues.

These enhancements occur because the company has become leaner and more responsive. Just as the dieter discovered a new mobility and new energy, the company discovers another opportunity—new revenues and profits. The value-managed enterprise has more than new skills; it has knowledge that can be leveraged in the marketplace, especially to satisfy customers even more. Firms that embrace the Wall Street Diet have opened a major gap between themselves and less able competitors; these companies begin to dominate their industries. Leaders such as Wal-Mart, Procter & Gamble, Toyota, Intel, Nike, and Dell testify to the values added through concerted, enterprise-wide efforts that result in increased revenues.

These leaders have created sales advantages that translate directly into increased profit because of the reduced costs. Sales fall cleanly to the bottom line as profit. Leaders gain these advantages through access to and use of knowledge across what becomes an intelligent value chain network. When that knowledge is combined with an effort to develop greater satisfaction with the most important customers, the advantage becomes a factor of differentiation.

Nike stands out in this respect as a firm that can take a customer request for a set of superstar athlete–branded shoes, look into its end-to-end network, and with high reliability know exactly where every part might be. From raw materials to goods in transit, the firm can track product movement and make sure it is at the point of need at the right time. Wal-Mart and Procter & Gamble are able to dramatically reduce out-of-stocks by using similar capabilities to ensure that a customer does not go to another store to find a product.

In this chapter, we will explore the opportunity to use the benefits of our diet to build sales, by linking together four topics to the revenue-enhancing side of the Wall Street Diet: advanced supply chain management, customer relationship management, technology application, and customer intelligence. By looking holistically at these topics, companies can develop integrated strategies and solutions for delivering products and services to key customers better than any competitor. When the effort is extended through technology to allow businesses to access vital parts of a database quickly and cheaply to meet a specific customer need, the advantages are unmatched.

The Wall Street Diet cannot be considered successfully applied unless profitable sales revenues have been generated as a result of the new lean configuration.

SUPPLY CHAIN MATURITY MATCHED WITH CUSTOMER INTELLIGENCE PROGRESS

As Exhibit 8.1 illustrates, customer relationship management (CRM) progress can be matched with the supply chain maturity model described in Chapter 3. Beginning in the mid-1990s, most firms progressed through the first levels of the supply chain evolution. They began with enterprise integration, where they made early savings through sourcing and logistics efforts, very little of which was passed on to the customer. It was at this level that most firms realized they needed a greater orientation toward customer satisfaction. The primary emphasis has been on cost reduction, with a risk that customer needs would be sacrificed for the sake of greater efficiencies.

EXHIBIT 8.1 Customer Intelligence Is Driven by the Convergence of Capabilities

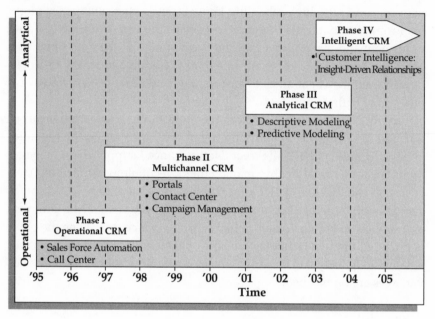

Next came Level 2 with multichannel CRM—satisfying customers through different channels (e.g., stores, a toll-free number, the Internet, etc.). Firms moved to operational excellence, where internal obstacles were conquered, and planning, order management, manufacturing skills, and inventory management became serious parts of the effort. During this time, many companies also progressed into a form of operational CRM with efforts geared toward satisfying customers as well as cutting costs. Sales force automation was used as companies learned they could use data to enhance the ability of sales representatives to help customers find extra values. Call centers came into vogue, as contact centers were established to match the needed services with what would truly help key customers.

Toward the end of that period, while in the second level of the effort, campaign management emerged. Firms learned they could ally themselves with key suppliers and customers to improve the results of special sales efforts. Tesco, the large UK supermarket firm, does this effectively with Nestlé. These firms collaborate on sales promotions for coffee or confections, for example, and achieve unusually high sales lifts by making certain the supplies are matched with customer demand by store. As a direct result of the collaboration, there are no out-of-stocks during these sales events.

At the beginning of the new century, firms that maintained a dedication to the supply chain effort moved into Level 3, or analytical CRM, the phase in which technology becomes a necessary component of customer satisfaction. They began working with their key partners to find the hidden values in the linkage that elude firms bogged down in an internal-only focus without external data sharing. During this period, these firms typically applied technology to increase the knowledge transfer available to business allies.

Using the Internet as the major tool of communication, these companies began to share valuable information with selected and trusted business allies, so that they could further improve their abilities to create and sustain new revenues. These allies learned they could share previously sacrosanct and proprietary customer, marketing, and consumption information to determine important trends jointly and build revenues together, without risking their organizations' futures. Customer data integration became a vital technique to assemble and use important knowledge on customers, consumers, and market trends to introduce customized solutions and offerings.

One major consumer products manufacturer worked intensively with a large retailer to share such knowledge, so both firms could consider consumer data, analyze trends, and evaluate customer comments. The two firms discovered they were confusing the consumer with too many product choices. Take detergents, for example. There were twenty or more ways a particular branded item could be purchased—from liquid to powder, from small to large sizes, with bleach or without, and so forth. When the two firms began to transfer data electronically on these products and worked their collective knowledge—on actual preferences, supply chain costs, and obsolescence—they found the offerings could be reduced closer to six choices, with the actual assortment throughout the store based on local consumer preferences. Both firms ended up selling more at higher margins to happier consumers. Building customer satisfaction for loyal customers increased business and profit for both partners.

A few businesses managed to progress into Level 4, or intelligent CRM, and became part of a value chain constellation, where valuable knowledge is used for mutual improvements. They moved further with analytical CRM and began to reap the benefits of a true customer intelligence environment. Here the nucleus firm in the center of the supply chain network joins forces with key partners and drives the network to apply technology and analyze customer knowledge together. Better decisions could be made on supply and delivery of just what was needed because the data explained what was actually in demand and in stock to make deliveries. The linked partners in this level overcome resistance to sharing important data and transfer knowledge, and the network appears unique to the customer.

John Deere stands out as an example of an organization that consistently ranks higher than its competition in customer satisfaction with that market group. This firm carefully analyzes what farmers really need and look for in farm implements, recognizing their often-limited resources. This information is fed directly into Deere's product development database to determine what products to design and deliver. Good customer intelligence yields satisfaction with more business and additional profit.

One important output during this part of the evolution became known as *demand chain management,* where the actual needs of the end consumers and customers were matched with the capability of the supply chain to meet those needs. Essentially, demand chain and supply chain converged, and the value-managed enterprises that emerged were better able to respond to what the market truly wanted. A major food manufacturer used this technique to increase sales lifts significantly on special sales events and promotions, often achieving 5 to 7 percent greater returns in test cases. Online visibility across the network allowed the firm to track movement from the beginning to end of its supply chain and get products to the point of need quickly, based on access to real-time consumption data.

Customer intelligence means you stop looking at mountains of data and gather the knowledge that needs to be analyzed to find answers.

The requirements supporting this evolution are not exactly novel. Improving profitable revenues with targeted customers and retaining their loyalty have been central tenets of business strategy for a long time. What is new is the use of a different kind of knowledge and information. With access to helpful knowledge buried in burgeoning databases, it becomes a modern art, enhanced through technology applications. When the effort is extended to integrating CRM systems with ASCM efforts and access to customer intelligence, a chance to differentiate a firm and its closest business allies appears.

CUSTOMER RELATIONSHIP MANAGEMENT— A CONTEMPORARY VIEW

In the current state of CRM, most markets are under pressure to show actual value for the necessary investments in time, resources, and capital. These efforts are complex, and the cost of integration across a business enterprise can be high. As a result, current views of the potential values are tempered by a need for immediate process improvement and bottom-line returns. When executed with enhanced processes and enabling technology applications to acquire, develop, and retain an organization's best customers, CRM becomes a powerful tool for increasing revenue and profit.

CRM has its roots in the idea that as a firm's supply chain moves toward maturity, it becomes more effective at both internal and external processing. It progresses from making the most of the best practices to achieve parity or better against competing firms, to the point where it adds values to the customer that are not found through other alternatives. Most of these techniques will require enabling technology and the sharing of vital knowledge with key external resources. Exhibit 8.2 depicts some of the features of an *intelligent value chain*, which becomes the end product of a successful ASCM/CRM technology-enabled effort.

Within the intelligent value chain, business allies are working together from a right-to-left perspective. They begin with what it takes to have a competitively advantaged network in the eyes of the ultimate consumer. They then work backward to determine what the upstream side of the value chain should be doing to achieve the desired superior conditions. They use the Wall Street Diet ingredients collaboratively to satisfy customers better. Together, the linked parties are working to find the best solutions and practices for all of the key process steps. Beginning with improved forecasting and the necessary linking processes, the network partners devote their best resources to find superior product development, the

EXHIBIT 8.2 The Intelligent Value Network

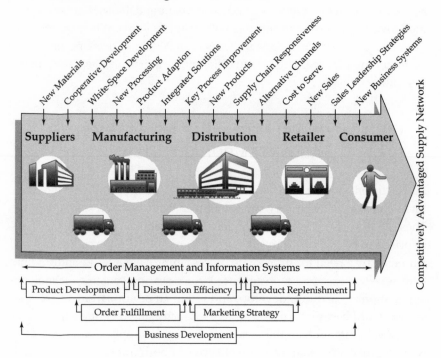

ultimate distribution efficiency, the best methods for product replenishment, jointly developed marketing strategies, and the best order fulfillment system. All these processes become industry-best practices—serving the customer. Along the way, they work collaboratively to find the best enterprise processes and become extremely effective at any point of handoff between supply chain constituents. In short, they are working in concert to make the Wall Street Diet work across the complete business enterprise.

Two requirements must be met as this intelligent value chain is constructed and nurtured. First, each participant in the network must have attained Level 3 or beyond in the supply chain maturity model with the ability to use disparate databases so that valuable knowledge can be extracted without compromising the security. Second, the enabling technology applications must be selected collaboratively and be functioning successfully across the end-to-end network processing. That means the collaborating business allies are working in concert, with each making valuable contributions to create the desired differentiation in the eyes of the most coveted customers.

THE VALUE OF CUSTOMER INTELLIGENCE

An important purpose lies behind the effort to establish greater customer intelligence. A single view of the customer can properly focus efforts across the business, improve customer interactions, reduce operational costs, and enhance revenue.

To begin, most organizations have multiple records and accounting for the same customer, without consistent information transfer across business units. Customers are treated inconsistently. The business body is not healthy.

Much time and effort are wasted collating reports and gathering information, much of it historical. Instead, the firm could analyze high-value information (demand trends) and knowledge (how to get the goods and services to customers faster than competitors). Much of the marketing effort to build demand is focused on mass market techniques, rather than the preferred targeted segments offering the most lucrative returns. Unable to concentrate on the right customer at the right time, with no predictive modeling capabilities, the firm spends corporate energies on low- instead of high-value customers. Service levels are clearly inadequate.

Solutions to these complications can add dramatically to the firm's performance, including such features as these:

- Data management personnel savings
- Faster call handling of inbound inquiries
- Prospect and customer solicitation savings
- Reduction in returned communications
- Improved data quality in critical operational systems
- Improved targeting for cross-sell, up-sell, retention, and acquisition campaigns
- Lower customer attrition rates

More important, the firm can now approach customer intelligence in a more contemporary manner. By today's standards, CRM has become the deployment of strategies, processes, and enabling technologies that are used to acquire, develop, and retain an organization's best customers. It includes understanding customer needs, the relative importance of each customer segment, and the best, most economical means to meet those needs. Within an environment focused on this view of CRM, strategy, processes, organization, and culture begin to revolve around a central focus dedicated to satisfying customers in the most appropriate manner and sustaining those with most strategic value indefinitely.

Healthy and effective processing has never had more meaning in this environment. Organizations that remain fragmented and operate in a stovepipe manner will never achieve the advantages being cited. They will be doomed to local optimizations within some business units and be prevented from achieving network process and systems optimization. Results from such systems as enterprise resource planning, CRM, and collaborative planning forecasting and replenishment will simply never be fully achieved due to process inefficiencies. In traditional diet terms, quick weight loss will not be maintained, and old habits will reappear, perhaps with greater strength.

Process design and enabling technologies, methodologies, and tools provide the greatest opportunity to increase corporate performance today. The drivers behind this return to a process focus, moreover, will be an enhanced customer-controlled environment, where customer satisfaction is the real end objective, with use of the Internet to create and control the sharing of valuable knowledge.

When ASCM and CRM converge in this advanced level of the evolution, some important characteristics will be apparent:

- Demand management and forecasting will be at improved levels, with actual need matched with capability to supply.
- Sales and operations planning will move to advanced planning and scheduling, where key suppliers and customers are participating in diagnostics and planning sessions to bring a reality to the planning and supply processing.
- Inventory management will be a network effort, in which the linked allies work to deliver the right goods to the point of need in the right quantities at the right time.
- Visibility into the end-to-end processing will be online, real-time, allowing the constituents to view what is taking place, track important events, and adapt the supply chain to ever-changing market conditions faster and more accurately than the competition.

- Event management will be at the highest possible level of effectiveness, as the reactions to any planned sales effort will be instantly relayed back to important upstream partners, so that they can react appropriately to actual event conditions and results.

In short, the customer's voice will be driving the supply chain, based on the segmentation that has determined the level of response necessary to satisfy the customers being served. This condition requires the firm to move through the four levels of the intelligent customer maturity model (Exhibit 8.3), developed by Alex Black, a senior partner at CSC.

In the first level, or the *starting gate*, the firm adopts a 360-degree view of the customer. Most processing involves excessive manual analysis and handling of the data. Use of the intranet, or internal communication system, has to be improved so there are no cultural inhibitors to building the most accurate, accessible knowledge on the most strategic customers.

In the second foundational level, where the firm begins to erect the *building blocks to success*, a common customer identification system is installed, and customer segmentation is used to separate the customer list by strategic value to the firm and profit to the firm.

EXHIBIT 8.3   Customer Intelligence Maturity Model

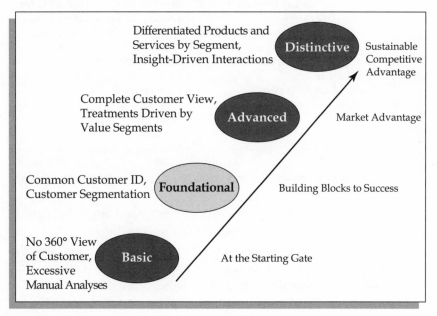

The following matrix has been used as a guide for such segmentation. It progresses from the low-strategic-value, low-profit customers (the "usual suspects"), to the high-strategic-value, profitable customers (those "to die for"). Within each block of the grid are comments intended to help the selection process.

High (Profits)	**For-the-Moment Buyers** • Returns diminish as service costs escalate • Spot buys can be lucrative, but spread over many suppliers • Firms show some willingness to pay for added values • Limited advancement possibilities • High cost to retain loyalty	**Winners — To Die For** • Returns low relative to cost-to-serve • Focus is on total value; balanced scorecard analyses to prove benefits • Firms provide resources to seek joint savings; offer help with joint selling efforts • History of mutual partnering, sharing in risk • Low cost to retain loyalty
Low (Profits)	**Usual Suspects** • Spot buyers; pricing is crucial to decisions • Will switch for any perceived, momentary lower cost • Will leverage volume frequently; apply auction techniques • Very limited advancement possibilities • Potential for third party fulfillment, sales automation	**Wannabes** • Lengthy relationships; have shown signs of loyalty while insisting on special servicing for which they are reluctant to pay • Low probability for increasing profits without innovative selling approach • Show some elements of partnership for joint profits • Have fit with firm's capabilities, value offerings but tend to have high cost-to-serve
	Low **Strategic Values** High	

Two types of analysis are then used to identify and target the highest-potential customers. A *profiling* tool is used next to determine who and where the best customers are and what they really need. In this "descriptive modeling" area, focus is brought to such elements as lifetime value, demographics, behavioral trends, and decile analysis.

A *targeting* tool is also used to determine how the firm identifies the right offer to the right customer at the right time. In this "predictive modeling" area, focus goes to propensity to churn higher sales, chances for cross-selling and up-selling, and the propensity to buy.

Returning to the maturity model framework (Exhibit 8.3), as a firm moves into the "advanced" Level 3 of the progression, Black advises that it should begin to build a *market advantage* through ASCM/CRM. Now the organization is working selectively with business allies and develops a complete customer view, with treatments and services matched with the value segments from the segmentation grid. Together, these allies link those components of the various databases that contain valuable customer information in a manner that protects internal security. The involved parties have agreed to what knowledge will be made available and for what purposes, and they have established a secure means of access.

In the "distinctive" level, a *sustainable competitive advantage* is the objective. Here, the nucleus firm in the extended enterprise and its allies are offering differentiated products and services matched with the needs of the various segments in the grid. Through the sharing and analysis of mutually provided information, insight-driven interactions are a part of the scheme. The joint analysis of the data being transferred over the extranet connecting the value chain constituents is providing knowledge unavailable to competing networks. As this model is considered, it is imperative that a firm desiring such an advanced position evaluates itself and determines where the organization and its network partners fall on the maturity scale. Then a determination can be made of where the firm needs to be, and the business partners can begin building a plan to achieve that position.

Market dominance comes about by knowing better than any other network how to offer meaningful solutions to the most important customers.

If the firm puts the same amount of effort into the revenue side of its business as it did on the cost side, it should gain a comparable improvement and a special reward. The improved self-esteem and confidence engendered in the employees should be an incentive to get customers and business analysts to better appreciate what has happened. By applying the enhancements gained through the cost side of the diet, the firm now should be more attractive to key segments of its customer base. If it then harmonizes its cost efforts with directed moves to increase sales, the circle is completed, and both top- and bottom-line results improve. The special reward is new revenues with the most desired customers.

Enhanced self-esteem should lead to a more positive attitude and stronger capability to impress customers and analysts. Just as a formerly obese person now gets appreciative glances on the beach because of the change in appearance, so a business will be more attractive by virtue of the improvements reported in the media, especially to customers willing to switch business to a firm that is now perceived to be healthier and more attractive.

SUMMARY

Our dieter has found a lifestyle characterized by greater flexibility, more choices, more freedom, and more movement. All these positive outcomes must be maintained in the diet regimen that has brought success so far. Life seems so much better.

Information to trim the fat and prosper abounds in most business organizations. The problem is that much of this knowledge is not used intelligently because it is stored in nonintegrated databases and rarely shared across internal business units or with business allies willing to help. Using valuable information forms the basis of customer intelligence, and it begins with a common definition of customers, a description of the tools to be applied, and the information integration architecture necessary to make the system a viable business enhancement process.

The overall objective of the Wall Street Diet should be to attain a position of market dominance by virtue of using customer intelligence to differentiate, in the customers' eyes, the deliveries from the network. This chapter has presented a framework that will lead to new revenues as well as optimized costs. The firm must analyze the tremendous amounts of customer data so that it becomes a source of customer knowledge and can anticipate and react to market conditions better than any competitor. Revenue generation will evolve in ways similar to those described in the maturity model used for supply chain progression. At all times, the business eye should be kept on metrics reflecting customer satisfaction, as well as improving operational efficiencies.

CHECKLIST FOR SENIOR MANAGEMENT

☐ Insist on using the benefits of the Wall Street Diet to enhance revenue. The cost improvements have been tremendous, but the greatest value lies ahead.

☐ Ensure that the entire network is focused on the end customer or consumer, and be prepared to share the rewards.

☐ Insist that each business unit conducts a market segmentation to identify the highest-priority customer groups and takes serious action to abandon those segments sapping business energy.

☐ Have plans prepared that match diet efforts with the customer segments where new revenues will be generated.

CHECKLIST FOR FUNCTIONAL MANAGERS AND DIET CHAMPIONS

☐ Select one customer or customer group from the customer segmentation analysis, and build a concerted sales campaign, featuring the benefits gained through the diet. Determine where special values, not normally found in the market, can be presented as a differentiating feature—shorter cycle times, better on-time delivery, higher fill rates, fewer returns, more perfect orders, and so forth.

☐ Construct a special sales campaign to bring those values to a few customers willing to allow you to advertise the improvements made, so that the campaign can be extended.

☐ Bring the customer directly into the loop, by offering to share some of the ideas and benefits from the diet, so that the customer can make similar gains.

☐ Choose a function within the business (e.g., IT). Sit down with this internal customer to explain how new capabilities are present, and use a partnering diagnostic lab to determine where they can add value for the internal customer. Document the improvements against a baseline level of performance, and take time to make at least an order-of-magnitude estimate of the impact on financial reports.

BEGIN WITH HEALTHY INGREDIENTS—
GET BEYOND THE CULTURAL ROADBLOCKS

For dieters to reach the final goal, two more issues must be addressed.

First, they need to change their *total* lifestyle. They may have had some success in reducing caloric intake or in avoiding certain kinds of foods. They may have given up snacking. At the same time, our dieters may not have taken up the exercise habit. Or, they may still be seasoning food with too much salt. The key to long-term, long-lasting success is to adopt a completely new lifestyle—one where good habits are completely ingrained.

The business similarly will need to look at the whole Wall Street Diet. There are implications for costs as well as revenue. Different tools are used, but it's important that they all be used. Most failures or failure-to-thrive with these disciplines occurred because the disciplines were adopted in a vacuum. This is no longer the case. The Wall Street Diet offers a comprehensive approach to the whole value-managed enterprise and supporting supply chain.

The second issue may be even more difficult. Let's assume our dieter is a middle-aged man. One of his old habits was to join colleagues for regular drinks and bar food. These choices are incompatible with his new dietary regimen. If his colleagues have no interest in adapting to some of the elements of the regimen, it's possible the dieter will bid his friends good-bye. Lifestyle changes mean just that. It means moving from the comfort of an old set of habits into a new comfort zone.

New support groups will emerge, just as new business partners within the network emerge. Key people within and outside the firm will become champions of the Wall Street Diet and its approaches.

Change will occur in almost every area. For a short time, almost everyone will experience some kind of discomfort until the new routines become comfortable.

As any firm approaches a major improvement effort, especially one involving a significant business transformation like the Wall Street Diet, two rival camps appear. There will be *advocates* calling for significant change and *cynics* resisting and worrying that a major transformation initiative will destroy progress already made. The advocates will cite problems with satisfying key stakeholders—for example, deplorable delivery and customer satisfaction situations. The calls for action may sound an alarm but are often poorly received by the cynics, who point out that past performance has sustained the firm. Conducting business in the usual fashion and allowing people to remain in a comfort zone permits the cynical business leaders to avoid having to alter long-standing strategies. Cynics favor slow, incremental change.

Differences between the two camps must be resolved, or the firm will not progress. A champion must appear, who will share a guiding vision that is compelling and will align the senior officers.

Warning: The Wall Street Diet is not about competing; it is about winning!

We stand with the advocates, as we have rarely found a business that could not significantly improve its performance in a number of areas. Most companies have some serious health problems. The Wall Street Diet is not about incremental change and sliding back into bad practices. It is about facing reality solidly and with purpose. The firm takes dramatic steps for future advantage, particularly in the eyes of key customers. An organization-wide improvement effort will lift all parts of a business to internal-best and then to predetermined industry-leading standards. As advocacy prevails, we find even the most reluctant firms can bring their weaker parts (business units or functions) to a slimmer and more agile state. As we have seen earlier, outsourcing may also be an option. The key is that the organization is only as strong as its weakest area.

CULTURAL INHIBITIONS MUST BE ANTICIPATED

No firm is going to succeed with our diet, however, without first gaining a consensus on where the business is operationally and what is missing. Those who will have responsibility for execution may have an image of what they would like the firm to become, but much more needs to be done. Because the Wall Street Diet will apply to business units, then the enterprise, and then the network, it is imperative to address the cultural issues across the entire span. The cynics must be identified and heard. Then, they may choose to become part of the change or eventually leave and be part of the history.

To show how to overcome resistance to the Wall Street Diet, we will use a concrete business example throughout this chapter. We will describe in detail an actual implementation, fraught with cynics and resistance, where advocates used the ideas forming the framework for the Wall Street Diet to reach unprecedented levels of improvement in a particularly difficult industry. We think you will have a better picture of how the diet's healthful ingredients fit together and become easier to implement.

APPLYING THE WALL STREET DIET
IN A DIFFICULT ENVIRONMENT

The Wall Street Diet will work for any firm in any business. However, to create the clearest example, we chose a company that had relied on improvements to market conditions (shorter supply so prices could rise) and capital investment (to reduce costs) to enhance return on investment.

The business was forest products (a cyclical industry), and the company had a diversified line of business units, including woodlands and harvested trees, dimensional lumber, logs and chips, kraft paper made both at company-owned mills and purchased from external suppliers, corrugating medium, shipping containers, folding cartons, waste paper processing, and specialty products, which included aluminum and plastic packaging. The firm had annual sales of approximately $5 billion and net profits that varied depending on market conditions (demand/pricing) from 2 to 5 percent of revenues.

Before the company considered this major improvement effort, it had conducted a variety of quality and productivity enhancement exercises, primarily on a business unit basis. None had used process improvements. Most of these efforts had produced documented improvements, essentially to annual yields (output/input) and waste reduction. The momentum had stalled, however, and wastes were creeping back to former levels. During the cross-organizational executive workshops arranged to achieve alignment around an improvement initiative, the attendees were challenged to reconsider current efforts. They determined that some of the existing techniques should be salvaged and included in any consolidated process improvement regimen. Other techniques could not be integrated and needed to be eliminated immediately.

Statistical process control techniques, manpower utilization, waste control, and just-in-time delivery were among the previously successful initiatives that would be included in the new, comprehensive effort. Excess inventories, long lead times, and percentage of rejected products (returns) were on the "need for quick improvement" list.

There were no consistent directives or final objectives, priorities for choosing new actions, or scorecards to document and track overall improvements. As an example of the symptoms, we found the primary emphasis throughout the organization was on product throughput, and most bonus plans were paid out on annual volume increases, regardless of the prices at which products were sold—symptoms of a push-oriented culture. Inventories across the organization had been increasing for ten years, as plants continued to make product whether demand existed or not.

Under a dynamic CEO (the champion), who became determined to force through the transformation, the decision was made (with almost complete alignment after the workshops) to undertake a company-wide improvement effort. The goal of this organization was to earn money at a rate that would ensure the company's viability in both the short and long term. The management committee decided the firm should develop a system of innovative business practices to provide a continually improving manufacturing process, with optimized use of resources and supply chain enhancement at the effort's center. This change would yield a 100 percent increase in earnings as the overall target. The metrics to determine success became new revenues, throughput, operating expenses, inventory, customer satisfaction (fill rate, on-time delivery, etc.), and earnings per share. To make certain the firm did not lose any gained ground and would sustain the improvements, a scorecard was created with industry benchmarks to ensure a competitive advantage.

ESTABLISHING THE NEED FOR A SIGNIFICANT CHANGE EFFORT

Our first challenge was to make the case for a significant change effort in the company. As expected, two camps quickly formed. The cynics consistently pointed to past achievements as evidence of having reached industry-best conditions. We knew this point was incorrect. "Take your effort to the competition" became a defensive cry—"they need it more than we do." Without an initial, well-accepted, and clear leadership vision of an improved future state, many listened to this cry, and acceptance of the status quo became the cultural imperative to overcome. Some of the most senior officers refused to accept any suggestion that an improvement effort could do more than nudge performance to a slightly higher plateau. Only more favorable market conditions or large infusions of new capital would have the desired dramatic effect being suggested, we were told.

Step 1 in the resolution was to introduce a case for action by introducing a compelling future state *vision*—a picture of the improved lifestyle. We decided to attack the cynics' camp by pointing to acceptable performance measurements that showed a gap between the firm's figures and those from more effective companies with similar business processes. When the final document was viewed from the top of the financial statement (revenues and revenue growth) through all cost entries to net profit before taxes, the analysis showed an opportunity to double earnings.

This approach got us closer to our objectives but not exactly where we wanted to be. Most of the executives either could not accept or did not want to accept the data being presented. A problem we have encountered often was at the heart of the resistance: denial. In many cases, the data show a large gap between performance in an area under the control of a high-ranking officer and what it could be with improved processing. Rather than accept the challenge to close the gap and add significant new earnings, the reaction is to deny the validity of the data. Upon further substantiation, the second line of defense is to claim the proposed improvement effort was not applicable for that particular part of the business. In cases of extreme denial, the solution is the CEO's mandating of forward progress.

Using the metrics we developed and placed under the direction of the CEO, we created pro forma statements of what the enhanced business condition could mean. He was energized by the view of a future state that showed double current profits. We presented the statements to all business units, senior managers, and the firm as a whole—like doctors explaining the value of weight loss within a changed lifestyle. Specific improvements would improve business profits and earnings per share. Conveniently, these were central elements in the existing bonus plan. A few malingering executives moved to the advocate camp when they saw the potential positive effect on their bonuses.

If you want an organization to support the rigors of the Wall Street Diet, you must present compelling financial and customer satisfaction improvements as the end results.

We had built a case for action that was embraced across the firm. Now we entered the second phase of establishing the need for the effort. We needed to create full *awareness* regarding the intentions of the change effort and the potential for positive impact. The resistance continued until most of the senior officers accepted what the transformation could do to their part of the business, to the company as a whole, and to their personal income. Building awareness meant bringing in reliable subject matter experts to document the gaps cited by the performance metrics and to review in greater detail how the change effort could improve all sectors of the business. These sessions were expanded into a series of executive workshops, where preliminary worksheets were completed depicting the financial impact that might be achieved through a specific list of actions. We now had the help of the managers themselves in designing the diet to be followed.

We had a case for action and full awareness of the issues. Gaining *alignment* came next, as we encountered difficulty bringing members of the two camps into a single view of what would become the largest change process ever undertaken by the firm. While we had broken down many of the stovepipes and silos of indifference, we still had influential people advocating too many different approaches to the solution. We knew only a unified effort, endorsed by all key executives, would succeed with this business. We did not move forward until we had endorsement across the business and a strong feeling that the alignment was complete. The CEO played a major role here.

BEGINNING WITH LEAN TECHNIQUES

The actual improvement effort started with the Toyota productivity system and Taiichi Ohno's teachings generally known as *lean initiatives*. We summarized his thoughts and excerpts from the Shingo books, which became required reading (about thirty pages). Eventually, most employees could quote the central concepts from memory.

Three ideas became pervasive before the effort went forward. First, the company wanted and would need total employee involvement, throughout all business units and supporting functions. Whatever was done would reflect cooperative actions and a concerted continuous team effort. The whole place was going to get lean.

Second, strong incentives for innovation would be offered and allowances made for calculated risks taken. The thinking was basic: Toyota was already demonstrating an ability to have employees submit thirty or more ideas per person in a single year. Our firm was generating less than one per employee. Toyota also tolerated calculated risks and had a superior advantage over domestic carmakers, who tend to punish failure. Our firm had been known for severely punishing failure.

To track progress, a third imperative was introduced: a simple and universal chart was to be created for every targeted process improvement, showing the base position, the challenging new target, and the steps, time frames, and accomplishments that would be made toward that goal. Progress was to be attained by moving from a lesser position (A) to a higher position (B), with documentation of the progress.

A final charge was added to the effort's charter, which was to keep the central focus squarely on satisfaction of true customer needs—internally and externally. The CEO was determined to make the firm more customer-centric, as a means of gaining a market distinction and eventually leading to revenue growth. The concurrent supply chain efforts would be part of a holistic business strategy with discrete but not opposing tactics. The end result would be greater customer satisfaction and the creation of new sales.

The name given to the effort was "Excellence in Manufacturing" (EIM), which the sponsors termed a logical evolutionary, customer-driven survival and sustenance strategy.

The specific requirements to be included in the EIM strategy were very similar to the Wall Street Diet. The firm was to lose weight and become healthier, more responsive, and more flexible by adopting business practices aimed at process optimization—getting the body into the best possible set of conditions and keeping it there. Included in this business regimen were the following ingredients:

- An integrated business approach that met the demands of changing marketplace conditions for each business unit, with as close to optimized operating conditions as possible
- An improvement process with a consistent business language, improvement specifications, and controlling metrics to ensure that progress was made and sustained
- An understandable priority of decision options so resources (primarily human) could be effectively allocated—the best skills being applied to the most important improvement efforts
- A process that would be continuous and generate further improvements
- A sustainable advantage generated in each business unit, or the unit would be subject to sale
- A concerted team effort that would involve as close to 100 percent participation as possible
- A continuous list of documented targeted accomplishments, maintained in the scorecard and promoted across the company
- Payouts to participants consistent with the documented savings generated (an acceptable ratio between bonus and net savings was determined and made part of the effort for hourly and salaried personnel)
- A central focus that would be on satisfaction of customer needs

The effort was augmented by a variety of quality techniques and applications. The basics of the Wall Street Diet were now in a formation stage.

Costs Became an Immediate Target

In a review of fundamental Ohno concepts, it was determined that for all products except specialty goods, the firm and its operating units had little direct impact on market prices. Therefore, the traditional formula of Selling Price = Costs + Profits had no meaning because the firm could not set the selling price. Rather, this company needed to work from the formula that said Profit = Selling Price – Cost. Since market conditions set the selling price, the profit target necessary to double earnings per share was used to stipulate what costs had to be achieved. Now the focus went to a very simple axiom from Ohno's counsel. All participants were to concentrate on the saying "True cost is the size of a plum seed."

The thinking behind the adage is that if one person could use just enough materials to make just enough products to satisfy one day's orders, the cost of such an effort would be close to the optimal costs, or the size of a plum seed. If that person made product for tomorrow, space would be needed for the extra material, the material would need to be handled extra times, and someone would be needed to keep track of the material.

Managers tend to bloat the size of the plum seed and then shave off a little and call it cost reduction. That practice must be discouraged. EIM was aimed at rooting out all extra costs so that a theoretical minimum, in many cases derived through productivity profiling, could be achieved. In dietary parlance, only healthy foods were to be ingested. Since the program was oriented around good throughput, that commodity was defined as gross sales less returns and operating expenses. For the purposes of execution, attention went to all the costs between sales and profit. No category of cost was exempt, and each business unit went through each line on its operating profit statement, approaching each entry as a candidate for improvement. The usual suspects appeared:

- Materials—raw, work-in-process, and parts; supplies; material handling
- Selling expense; administration costs
- Freight
- Labor
- Energy; utilities
- Depreciation

Essentially, a full organizational effort was launched to find any and all improvement opportunities.

REACHING BEST PRACTICE: A HARD BUT BENEFICIAL EFFORT

We discovered early on that opportunities were very close at hand. In each business unit, specific plants or functions had achieved a healthier position than others within the same group or other parts of the firm. Significantly, none of the better practices were being shared. Within the functions across the company, we found clear differences in the way standard operations were being performed—order entry, forecasting, planning, scheduling, customer service, billing, payments, and so forth.

Documenting the best practices became considerably easier than getting other parts of the business to adopt these practices. When one team, for example, took the time to find and document the absolute best way to enter orders—without error or need for reconciliation—it took over a year to get that practice executed across the firm. When automated purchasing was instituted for nondirect categories and showed double-digit savings, it took almost two years to get all business units to implement the procedures.

Working within the plants was a bit easier, because of the willingness of the hourly personnel to accept what became improved processing techniques. One example explains how this was accomplished. In general, the business was characterized by large capital equipment that required being set up for specific product specifications. The time to make the setups or to change from one order to another became an early improvement effort. To get as close to the plum seed as possible, an intense effort was made to use productivity profiles to identify the best crew on each of the major machines, by virtue of their ability to make quality setups and changeovers in the lowest time. The crews, for example, who could set up a flexography printing press and generate quality product in the shortest interval were identified by site, shift, and Social Security numbers. Consider that the times for a changeover varied from less than twenty minutes to several hours, for the same type of job.

When these best teams were found, another effort was made to document what the crew members did that resulted in the company-wide best practices. Teams interviewed these crews; observed their productivity profiles, procedures, and actions; and even filmed them during actual set-ups. These films, with the supporting documentation of the element times and best practices, were circulated to other plants operating similar equipment. The usual resistance based on the claim that "We're different here!" was quickly subdued, and efforts were launched to move toward the best practices. Surprises occurred along the way. As the best teams were filmed, their changeovers improved as well, and we began seeing times well under fifteen minutes. As other crews began to accept the better practices, they pointed to techniques the best crews were *not* applying.

Based on the idea that even better practices were possible, films of the best crews were sent to the equipment manufacturers, which quickly called attention to yet further improvements that could be made. Across the company, the discovery was made that operators and helpers, personnel in virtually every function, were trained by those who formerly performed the same work, not by the machine manufacturers. Mostly, we found the operators and helpers, clerks, and office personnel had developed their own standard operating procedures. Bad habits were being institutionalized. In the case of the printers and paper machines, the manufacturers sent qualified personnel to retrain the worst crews, bringing productivity profiles to much higher levels and eventually creating truly best-practice films and instructions to be disseminated across the organization. Similar efforts paid dividends in office areas as well as plant environments. The organization improved in spite of itself.

BUSINESS UNITS USING THE DIET SET THE PACE

The effort gained in sophistication as EIM became a part of the dietary regimen. A few business units led with early acceptance of the principles within the Wall Street Diet. In one large operation, seven-color gravure printing presses were used to manufacture long runs of folding cartons for products such as cake mixes, detergents, and breakfast cereals. Changeover times usually ran a full shift or eight hours. That was the time required to clean the printing cylinders, remove the cylinders, and set in place new cylinders for the next run. Essentially, on a three-shift basis, the printing presses were available only 67 percent of the time.

Using changeover improvements techniques, the study team in this factory determined that the problem stemmed from the need to change the six or seven color units that were used on the printing press after completion of a run, and then setting and adjusting these units for the next run, all done while the press was idle. If the company could invest in a duplicate set of printing units—the large gravure cylinders—the crews could preset the next run, while the current run was being completed. This move was approved and resulted in the shortening of the changeover time to less than sixty minutes by doing most of the setup while the press was running.

In the same factory, the improvement idea caught on, and EIM moved faster than normal, leading to especially favorable changes with raw material storage and paper machine operations. Paper machines are large, capital-intensive units that produce big rolls of paper that can be sold to paper converters or cut to size for a variety of uses, such as the internal folding carton operation. Since this was a recycling plant, the raw material was basically waste paper. Outside the plant, almost two acres were devoted to the storage of waste paper supplies, with a turnover of about one time per year. Inside the plant, three paper machines produced what amounted to a fixed rate of tons per day.

The first effort was on the raw material storage and led to a technique that became a standard part of the EIM effort, called the *yellow tape experiment*. The type of yellow tape placed at accident scenes was used to segregate the outside storage area into four quadrants. These quadrants contained equal amounts of wastepaper and were marked A, B, C, and D. The new rule was that for ninety days, material would only be drawn from Sector A. The idea was to have the suppliers of waste paper deliver on a just-in-time basis to supply the needs of the pulping machines, without placing the raw materials into storage. If more material was needed, Sector B could be used, or C or D. After six months (because the managers had trouble believing the results of the experiment), Sectors B, C, and D were abolished. Eventually, all outside storage was eliminated, replaced by a small interior section for raw material storage. All other supplies went directly from the delivery cars and trucks to the paper-making equipment.

Inside the plant, an issue with the paper machines was quickly identified. Teams assigned to increase productivity used the productivity profiles that pointed to downtime as the major reason for what amounted to poor machine utilization. Deeper analysis led to the identification of maintenance on the machines as the root cause. Of an older vintage, the machines had reached the point where plant personnel were accustomed to taking significant downtime for repairs and replacements of key parts. The profiles indicated the three machines averaged no better than 50 percent run time. By instituting a more effective preventive maintenance program and using the best parts from three machines on two units, the plant was able to produce more tons per day with two machines.

DIETARY FUNDAMENTALS APPLIED AS ENHANCEMENTS

With so much improvement being documented, and to help the organization with the transformation that was ensuing, all personnel were required to attend team problem-solving sessions and root cause analysis training. A variety of techniques, including statistical process control, failure modes and effect analysis, ISO standards, and other tactics were covered. Special attention was given to crew and supervisory training to emphasize problem solving with managers as coaches and to achieve full participation among employees. Prizes were awarded to operations with the highest number of acceptable ideas per employee and for the best new practices introduced.

Inventory became a special area of concentration. It represented the money invested in buying things that were intended for sale. Inventory was redefined as investments waiting to be profits that should be delivered as soon as possible and just-in-time to meet customer needs. The waiting time was to be minimized as well as the invested working capital. Inventory concealed problems in the manufacturing system. The question asked at every discussion on inventory was not how much inventory was necessary but "Why is the inventory necessary?" Instructors made certain those in attendance at these sessions understood the effect that inventory had on profits, net assets employed, working capital needs, and carrying costs. By including the interest on working capital, the cost of space and material handling, spoilage, obsolescence insurance, and accounting, the total carrying cost was set at 12 percent per annum, and bonuses were added to the executive compensation system for reductions in base levels.

When the preliminary training was completed, teams were dispatched at every location and office function to build prioritized lists of potential improvements. These lists had to contain a reasonable estimate of the cost to implement and the benefits to be received. Kanbans, or carts with raw materials and parts, were used to restrict the amount of materials moving to any work station, since a new kanban could not be delivered until the crew was working from the bottom layer of the cart. Signboards were attached to these carts to indicate when the user was reaching that layer and needed replacement stock. *Poka-Yoke* lights—red lights intended to indicate a process problem—were set up on assembly line operations, so any crew member could shut down the line, turn on the flashing red light indicating a problem with the system, and have personnel quickly assemble to find the problem and solution.

All of these techniques derived from instructions in the Toyota lean manufacturing system. Zero inventories became the marching order. A quest ensued for constant improvement through imaginative attention to the overall task and minute details. One element was stockless production, the producing machine center orders material as needed. Another was load smoothing, balancing production schedules with actual demand so good materials are delivered just-in-time for the needed use, exactly when needed in the right quantity. Together these measures reduced the need for extra supplies. Balanced flow resulted in most cases as the focus on bottlenecks eliminated most manufacturing constraints.

Quality was not overlooked in the improvement effort; rather, it became a central feature, used to deliver what the customer expected and to reduce cost through elimination of materials and processing wastes. High quality was a requirement for process optimization, and any bad quality would only make the bottlenecks worse. Quality was part of the entire process. Doing things right the first time to achieve zero defects was the guiding mantra. Under these conditions, the ideal manufacturing system would accomplish the following:

- Produce what the customer wanted and needed
- Produce at the rate customers needed to be supplied
- Produce with perfect quality—create perfect orders
- Produce with close to zero lead time
- Produce without waste of labor, material, or equipment
- Produce with zero idle inventory

Virtually all teams began by creating process maps to focus investigations. Raw materials became an early category, and many of the study

can be applied enough to have a distinct effect. At key points in the process, you could see how suppliers and customers did participate. Champions, advocates, and cynics will appear in the network. The key is to create the focus, tools, and urgency to convert cynics or find new partners.

CHECKLIST FOR SENIOR MANAGEMENT

☐ Listen to cynics as well as the advocates, but create a single, unified approach. The greatest leverage comes from concentrated effort.

☐ Be prepared to challenge every objection, and do not tolerate excuses. There is no process, no area of the business that should not be investigated. Profits are hiding everywhere.

☐ Keep a scorecard on results, and celebrate the improvements.

CHECKLIST FOR FUNCTIONAL MANAGERS AND DIET CHAMPIONS

☐ Find a business unit or independent company that wants to "go on a diet."

☐ Give the change effort a catchy name, such as the New Organization Diet, Excellence through Dieting, Getting Lean and More Effective, or the Lean Solution. The name will help solidify the effort, but remember that just having a name is like just saying you're on a diet.

☐ Circulate *The Wall Street Diet*, but take the extra time to summarize the key points that have the most relevance for your firm.

☐ Start on the cost side.

☐ Bring in expertise, especially to provide guidance and create awareness.

☐ Use the partnering diagnostic lab described in the appendix to establish opportunity areas and early actions.

☐ Summarize key works from the quality, lean, and supply chain management literature for everyone to use. It will help create a shared foundation.

☐ Look for possible actions in every chapter of this book.

☐ Keep a sharp focus on ways to involve others in the network.

10

MAINTAIN THE GAINS—TURN THE DIET INTO A SUCCESSFUL BUSINESS PLAN

Our dieter has come a long way. At the beginning was a medical or personal need to reduce weight and develop a new lifestyle. The first step was developing a set of measurements to set a baseline and analyze what needed to be done. Then, better nutrition was combined with better flow within the body to ensure the right nutrients were getting to the right places at the right time. Each part of the dieter's lifestyle was examined, including assessing support groups, and changes were made in each area to bring those areas needing improvement into alignment with all other areas. Our dieter found experts to provide help in developing the healthier, leaner lifestyle. New measures confirmed the progress and pointed to even greater success. Instead of random fads, an integrated approach provided strength and structure.

All of these elements were integrated into a healthier lifestyle. And, people notice. Our successful dieter moves more easily and has much greater flexibility. Individual successes have built on each other to create a changed and dynamic person.

The business following the Wall Street Diet has made the same kind of transformation. New measurements, tools, visions, and dedication were used throughout the firm and its strategic allies. Powerful disciplines—advanced supply chain management, lean management, quality management, strategic outsourcing, technology, and fresh perspectives on the customers—were harnessed to create a new kind of enterprise. Just as the dieter developed a new, healthier lifestyle, the firm is a stronger, more flexible, and more profitable competitor. The new enterprise leads the industry.

It is time to consider how this fresh strength and health are maintained. The Wall Street Diet is sustainable. Even more, the successes achieved provide a platform for even more profit and leadership.

157

One of the features of the Wall Street Diet is that it is a plan. It provides the strength and structure to anticipate the future and capitalize on the present. We have also seen that the network provides new input on consumers, the supply chain, customers, and markets. In this chapter, we will examine how to use these newfound strengths and knowledge assets to create an even more successful future.

Every business is wise to undertake periodic audits to ensure that its competitive position is not eroding. Like a person visiting a respected clinic for a thorough physical checkup, the business undergoes controlled and valid health tests to determine that the best physical condition is being maintained.

Consider a few basic questions. Do some of your competitors occasionally react to market conditions and expectations of valued customers faster than your organization? Have one or more competitors responded to a key customer with a customized solution that you have overlooked? Does at least one competitor seem to make a profit on business that you are prepared to throw away? Have you been caught short by an innovative market approach by another firm?

If you answered yes to any of these queries, solvable problems might be lurking within your infrastructure. Perhaps the problem is that you are still expecting the same performance from machinery, equipment, job skills, technology, and systems that have served you in the past. Or could it be that you need a refreshed approach to expecting and receiving higher performance through a changed methodology and business discipline? We find more often than not that the latter question is the one needing an answer.

The best of companies have applied dietary elements to enhance already-commendable performance.

OPTIMIZATION AND MARKET DOMINANCE REQUIRE NEW THINKING

Reviews and audits should validate the current business health and focus on how to achieve enhanced business performance. The Wall Street Diet provides the foundation and tools to create a viable business strategy and action plan that ensures market dominance. That requires integrating the diet across the whole enterprise network and using the benefits to increase new revenues. The end result is a dramatic improvement to enterprise profits, no matter the current state of earnings.

This new level of flexibility and profit at a major clothing manufacturer and retailer illustrates our theme. If your firm were in the business of supplying millions of garments to a very demanding consumer segment, hardly anything is more important than being in front of what is in demand. Success depends on making lightning-quick responses and having the right products at the right place and time. That is precisely what Zara, a designer, manufacturer, and retailer owned by Inditex group, has been doing. It made significant changes to its supply chain, reaching near-optimized conditions. In an industry marked by designers spending months planning the next season's offerings, Zara uses its people, technology, and systems to get new products designed and into stores in just two weeks. As just one feature of the transformation achieved by this firm, Zara sales clerks send feedback information to designers via wireless PDAs, so the designers can make adjustments and send them electronically to factories in northern Spain.

The transformation began of necessity, when owner Amancio Ortega thought he might lose his company in 1975 when a German retailer canceled a large order for lingerie. Out of desperation, Ortega opened a retail shop near his factory in La Coruña, Spain, and sold the goods himself under the name Zara. From that beginning, the firm has expanded to include 650 stores in fifty countries, with annual net income increases of 20 percent.

At the heart of this phenomenal growth is Ortega's simple business philosophy: "Control what happens to your product until the customer buys it. In adhering to this philosophy, Zara has developed a superresponsive supply chain. Because it can offer a large variety of the latest designs quickly and in limited quantities, it collects 85 percent of the full ticket price on its retail clothing, while the industry average is 60 percent to 70 percent" (Ferdows, Lewis, and Machuca 2004: 106).

Following a process similar to the Wall Street Diet, Zara has worked hard to reduce its costs while creating a supply chain system intended to grow new revenues as the firm enjoys unprecedented industry margins. The company outsources about half of its production needs, letting other firms manufacture the simpler lines. Zara transfers critical information about customers' reactions from shoppers to designers electronically in real time. It can track the transfer of materials and finished product across every process step in its supply chain. Technology enables its streamlined processes and communications.

The message is fundamental: Whether as a supplier, manufacturer, distributor, or retailer, the problems and solutions that differentiate a business must be constantly reviewed and efforts made to find improvements. With a distinguishing solution, the results are then translated into a definite strategy and operating plan to capitalize on the effort. With so much riding on being competitive and considered a cut above the competition, this move cannot be made casually. Firms determined to go forward with the Wall Street Diet should integrate the concepts into their planning as part of a controlled risk effort. Then, a coherent strategy defines the expected end position for the effort.

At the same time, the diet must not be considered as just an experiment in progress. Once the costs and benefits are better understood, and a strong case for action has been developed and accepted by senior management, it must be translated as well into a marketing plan. Applications are defined, and timetables for execution are established to achieve a reasonable return on investment.

Developing such a strategy and action plan requires the following elements:

- Identifying the costs, delivery enhancements, potential savings, and effect on customer satisfaction—making at least an order-of-magnitude assessment of the costs and benefits across an extended enterprise
- Defining the steps to execute a meaningful strategy and the relationship within the greater business strategy, operating plan, and supply chain model being pursued—explaining to key stakeholders what the firm plans to do and how it will affect the current and future business posture
- Exploring opportunities to pilot elements of the diet with selected trading partners to identify improvements and shared benefits
- Listing the functions and services that acceptance and deployment of the diet can bring to the business and its supply chain strategy, including tactical and strategic issues—noting where value can be added beyond satisfying key customer mandates
- Beginning documentation of the expected financial impact that will derive from deployment of the diet, starting with controlled

experiments and pilot tests to provide meaningful metrics—all of which helps you get your hands on what the future state might really look like and how it will affect profits.

STEPS TOWARD A WALL STREET DIET STRATEGY

The first step in developing a Wall Street Diet strategy should define, confirm, and refine the common set of business requirements that the firm must satisfy. These should reflect the changed conditions of the firm, and the requirements should include expectation of the investors and network.

The second step is to develop a conceptual framework depicting a possible improved future state. To develop this information, the company should identify the key stakeholders to be affected by adoption of the diet and decide how success will be defined and measured.

Exhibit 10.1 illustrates the processes involved in forming such a strategy. It begins with a *market analysis*. Industry imperatives define the demands of the intended customers at the present and in the near- and long-term time frames. This includes an honest appraisal of the positives and negatives of the company. A review of what competitors might be doing or planning should be included. It is essential to anticipate technology change or adoption and the impact of capital changes within the industry. The firm will examine information across the entire enterprise network to analyze customers and how their needs are being met. This new information is the key to understanding the real needs. The market analysis must reflect what is going to be a part of the business future.

Every business seeking to create a strategy based on the Wall Street Diet needs to answer five critical questions here and throughout the balance of the strategy development process:

- How sustainable is the business? How much and what part might be at risk if the firm does not implement some form of optimization strategy as a business practice in our industry or market?
- How capably can our existing processes adapt to the changes, meet the expected needs and demands of the market, and satisfy key customers?

EXHIBIT 10.1 Strategy Process

Industry Imperatives	Cost and Benefit Analysis	Opportunities and Threats		Operating Model
Competitive Analysis	Effect on Market Position	Target Market Positions	Strategic Decision	Technology Road Map
Technology Impact	Current Value Proposition	Winning Value Proposition		Organization Design
Customer Analysis	Business Strategy	Synthesize Strategy		Business Plan
Market Analysis	**Business Analysis**	**Value Propositions**		**Operating Plan**

- What is the cost/benefit of implementing the diet?
- How can the diet be used to enhance key processes within the supply chain?
- What is the best strategy to succeed and add value for all constituents?

The answers to these queries will help establish the background against which any decisions will be made.

The second step develops a *business analysis* that applies the answers to these questions and begins to fit the emerging concepts with anticipated market conditions. The firm starts with an outline of whatever is known about costs and benefits, drawing on what came out of the first step. Consideration must be given to the anticipated effect on market position for having or not having optimized supply chain capabilities.

Then the firm identifies the current *value proposition*—the message being delivered to customers regarding exactly what value is added to the relationship by dealing with the firm and buying its products and services. An analysis is made of what message is being brought to the marketplace, to determine whether it needs modification or, more correctly, how the new strategy can be successfully harmonized to appear as a logical extension of the current business approach. Now the business strategy starts to unfold as an extension of the current strategy and *operating plan*.

VALUE PROPOSITIONS MUST DRIVE THE STRATEGY

When value propositions are considered as the third step in the strategy process, a deep and frank review is made of the opportunities and threats posed by adoption or rejection of the Wall Street Diet. Now the firm considers targeted market positions and how the opportunities and threats will directly affect important segments, using value propositions that make sense to the key customers. The firm gains a distinctive advantage and eventually achieves market dominance using these value propositions.

The most important part of the exercise is to use the improvements gained through deployment of the Wall Street Diet to develop winning value propositions that secure the desired market positions and provide a reasonable return on the effort. With these values in hand, the firm then packages the strategy into simple selling points, understandable across the business, and begins codeveloping an execution plan with key network constituents. Upon thorough review and most likely many iterations, a set of strategic decisions are then made to guide the rollout and deployment, including risk-mitigating pilots and tests to prove the value of the chosen concepts.

Make certain the rigors of the Wall Street Diet support the value propositions being offered to the customers.

Connecting the effort in a consistent framework across all business units and functions within the company is critical to success with this step. In that way, a systematic approach can be provided to strategy formulation and execution throughout the firm. This systematic approach is only possible as a result of the Wall Street Diet in creating the enterprise network. Our experience shows developing the best value proposition generates the debate and open discussion to align the optimization effort and prioritize the actions to be taken. Moreover, it drives the choices that identify the new core competencies, creates focus around those competencies, and leads to the action that satisfies customers.

Action Steps

The firm should then move through a specific action step development process, as illustrated in Exhibit 10.2. The first step is to perform a value proposition diagnostic. The enterprise must go through a review of the current values being presented in the market to determine whether the threshold levels are high enough to draw a customer's attention away from competitors. The key is to determine the current level of performance for each proposition considered. Every business has its enablers and constraints in choosing viable propositions, so care must be taken to gain an honest opinion, often requiring the use of trusted external advisers to bring objectivity to the conversation.

In Step 2, the firm reviews its performance against a scorecard that identifies the gaps between as-is conditions and existing industry benchmarks. There is no room here for wrong conclusions. The chosen value proposition must be executed to industry leadership levels, and the gap needing closing must be clear as well.

Step 3 requires identifying and confirming strategically the most important proposition for market differentiation and dominance. This move requires a thorough consideration of industry structure and practices, competitors' capabilities, and so forth. The current employee skills and capabilities are also reviewed, as well as the enterprise's access to capital and technology.

In Step 4, the firm decides how to take action to close any important gaps between existing performance and industry standards. It is important to evaluate which propositions major industry competitors have chosen and how they are executing. Keep in mind that choosing a different proposition could provide the basis for market distinction.

Step 5 moves on to using the actions to attain a position of industry leadership with the chosen proposition, while pruning actions in other areas as necessary.

Finally, Step 6 is used to review the opportunities to pursue leadership with another proposition. A pilot test may be needed to verify some of the conclusions drawn.

EXHIBIT 10.2   Value Propositions—Action Steps

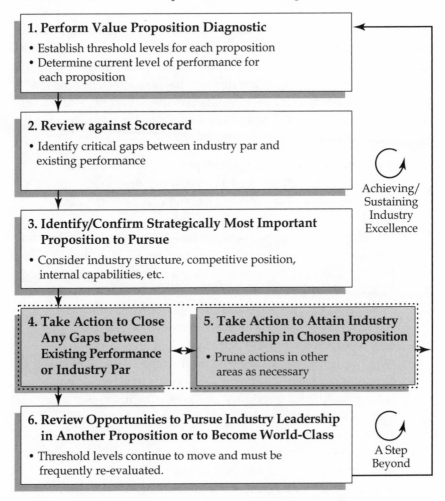

1. Perform Value Proposition Diagnostic

• Establish threshold levels for each proposition
• Determine current level of performance for
  each proposition

2. Review against Scorecard

• Identify critical gaps between industry par and
  existing performance

**3. Identify/Confirm Strategically Most Important
Proposition to Pursue**

• Consider industry structure, competitive position,
  internal capabilities, etc.

**4. Take Action to Close
Any Gaps between
Existing Performance
or Industry Par**

**5. Take Action to Attain Industry
Leadership in Chosen Proposition**

• Prune actions in other
  areas as necessary

**6. Review Opportunities to Pursue Industry Leadership
in Another Proposition or to Become World-Class**

• Threshold levels continue to move and must be
  frequently re-evaluated.

Achieving/
Sustaining
Industry
Excellence

A Step
Beyond

Using pilot test results or feedback from a customer council, the firm creates a modified business plan that reflects the new operating model. The new model adapts the existing model and includes a technology road map to guide implementation of the Wall Street Diet strategy. Organizational design changes are documented and explained, and a final business plan is blessed by all key stakeholders. Only then can execution begin in earnest. However, it is important to accept early in the planning process that this is a plan that must be constantly updated with new information gathered from further tests, proof of concepts, new market data, and any changed customer requirements.

During the development process and as the final strategy is revealed, the firm should begin listing the functions and services that an optimization effort can enhance. We recommend beginning with the functions and process steps in the supply chain that will be most affected. A review of the current process map for the business provides direction, and the firm can select its starter kit of potential improvements. We like to include the following functions:

- The customer order management process—where the lean features of the Wall Street Diet can improve the accuracy of incoming data and enhance the transfer of data from point to point
- Inventory planning and management—where the diet will reduce inventories (raw materials, work-in-process [WIP], subparts, and finished goods) by being able to identify the needed quantity and location of all goods in the end-to-end supply chain network
- Purchasing, procurement, and strategic sourcing—through reduced costs generated through lower embedded total costs, selective outsourcing, and automated sourcing procedures
- Manufacturing, fabricating, and production—because of lower handling costs, manufacturing costs, better tracking of supplies without calling for duplicates, and greater ability to perform under a kanban or advanced just-in-time delivery system
- Warehousing and distribution—with significantly lower cost due to reduced handling and the need to verify contents, locations, and availability of supplies and finished goods
- Transportation management—because of fewer emergency shipments, better cross docking, and fuller loads by knowing exact locations and readiness for pickup
- Customer response and calls for service—through elimination of the bulk of requests to find missing products or to better match actual demand with what is in the supply chain
- Customer billing and accounts payable—to improve the speed of collections and to reduce some of the current deductions and invoice reconcilement process

From a general viewpoint, among the more obvious values that might enhance these functions and services, we suggest the following:

- Values that can be added to existing core competencies that will result in sustained or increased revenues—such as transparency across the supply chain processing so that movement of goods can be identified and tracked anywhere, and duplicate or redundant steps or inventories avoided. Customers no longer need to guess at what is being delivered and can make changes without disrupting a supply chain.
- Alignment of the supply chain effort, using the Wall Street Diet as an enabler with the company's business objectives, so that key customers do not feel threatened during the transformation and develop additional backup sources of supply. By positioning the improvements from the diet as an extension of previously successful systems, most customers will exhibit more patience during the inevitable execution learning curve.
- Establishment of a consistent communication message that drives successful implementation and elicits further development of payback features. Everyone will be aware of the strategy, expected impacts, timetables, and elements of risk. In that way, each affected party can do its planning with the understanding of what might or might not develop as deliverables.
- Reduction of any potential gaps in expected performance that could radically erode market position or put the firm at risk from more adept competitors
- Development of a go-forward framework to minimize the inherent risks—through pilots, tests, and direct experiences to show the actual costs and benefits

BUILD A FINANCIAL CASE FOR ACTION

The next step is to go beyond order-of-magnitude cost and benefit estimates to develop an actual financial case for action. The question at this point is, Why are we going through the proposed set of activities supporting this Wall Street Diet strategy? The answer must provide a reason for developing, selling, and delivering an optimization-based solution or system to customers who demand high performance and who may be unsure of the benefits. Where costs are still unknown and new technologies are expected to have an impact, reliable ranges can be used. The purpose is to document what will be encountered, so the risks can be evaluated and controlled. Pilots and tests, of course, can be a part of this effort, to make the uncertain become more concrete.

During this part of the effort, the focus should be kept on business process improvement to get the processes correct. Technology takes a subordinate position to enhance the processing. This will continue as the optimization strategy progresses and the enterprise aligns along the strategies.

A firm should always take a holistic look at its business operations. The Wall Street Diet plays a vital role in completing and enhancing the business processes and creating leading systems. The best advice is to create self-funding opportunities early that meet the normal return guidelines applied to other investments. These first projects should generate short-term paybacks through labor cost reductions, capital avoidance, better asset management, inventory shrinkage, lower out-of-stock costs, and customer service improvements.

THE EXECUTION PLAN ESTABLISHES THE PILOTS AND ROLLOUT

When the strategy is formalized as a vital link in the greater business strategy and operating plans, the firm is ready to begin implementation. The execution plan that supports this phase should include setting up pilots for testing and verification. We advise that these pilots should be well defined and relatively quick. Three months is usually more than adequate to test the pilot hypothesis and gain enough information to make adjustments to the deployment plan. To minimize the risk, these pilots could also include simulations of expected conditions so potential results can be determined before putting too much at stake. For example, a consumer goods manufacturer could work with a retailer and use simulation techniques to pilot the introduction of a new product for a particular consumer group. Test results can be developed without actually introducing goods into the market. Acceptance or rejection depends on simulated responses. With the accumulation of the test results, acceptance and rejection will be based far less on simple compliance and speculation, and more on elements supporting the new strategy and guaranteeing a reasonable return on investment.

And what about results? One firm stands out as a prime example of what can be accomplished with the rollout of the Wall Street Diet. Toyota has applied its lean production system in many places, but none with more stellar results than at its Georgetown, Kentucky, facility where the original challenge was to sell the system's inherent concepts. Following a difficult transition period, in which the ideas and techniques were discussed with and sold to the employees, efficiency and quality standards rose continuously until they now "rival those of factories in Japan" (Chandler 2005: 78).

Similar accomplishments have been recorded across the enterprise as it has parlayed its version of the Wall Street Diet into unprecedented achievements. On the results side, Toyota's model lineup features some of America's most sought-after cars. The firm's hybrids, for example are ahead of all other competitors. Toyota's share of the U.S. market reached 12.2 percent in 2004, up from 6.4 percent in 1986, having already passed Ford as the number two global carmaker. Earnings, moreover, reached $10.3 billion in fiscal 2003, eclipsing the profits of General Motors, Ford, DaimlerChrysler, and Volkswagen combined.

Is the firm going to rest on its laurels and risk sliding backward? Not according to CEO Fujio Cho, who stated during the January 2005 international auto show in Detroit that running Toyota is less like driving a car than "trying to pull a handcart up a steep hill. There's always a tremendous danger if we relax, even for a moment; we could lose momentum and be thrown to the bottom" (Chandler 2005: 80). Obviously, the leader intends to maintain its position and will continue to carry the tenets of the Wall Street Diet to further optimization.

This is a lesson for all leadership enterprises.

Even with industry-leading capabilities, Toyota never ceases to search for other applications of its lean production system—to further enhance its performance.

Executives at Toyota take the matter seriously. The dilemma from their view is how to maintain the pace of progress without diluting the results. The solution is to continue the training in the Toyota production system and ongoing improvement at an accelerated rate. As an example of what can be accomplished, "At the Tsutsumi plant in Toyota City, 6,600 employees working two shifts on two separate production lines can turn out 500,000 vehicles a year in eight model variations at a rate of one per minute. It is a ballet of astonishing precision, enhanced by a myriad of [sic] tiny improvements on the factory floor" (Chandler 2005: 82).

CONTEMPORARY BUSINESS MODEL

As we consider turning the Wall Street Diet into a business plan, we must not forget the importance of including the enabling technology. A key component in the dietary plan is software that allows the linked businesses in the extended enterprise to share valuable information and knowledge pertinent to accomplishing the healthier lifestyle.

This case study involves Manhattan Associates, Inc., a major supplier of supply chain software, and a large distributor of food service products with a very complex supply network. The distributor handles everything from poultry, meat, and fish to produce and frozen entrées. The network encompasses every link in the life of such products, from farmers and other suppliers to thousands of customers.

Manhattan is very active in advanced supply chain management, providing a number of integrated solutions across a wide array of industries, including warehouse management, distributed order management, reverse logistics management, radio frequency identification (RFID), labor management, and transportation management systems. Seven of the ten largest North American warehouse management groups use Manhattan solutions.

As part of its supply chain improvement effort, the distributor decided to augment its capabilities and increase value across the end-to-end processing with suppliers and customers. To accomplish that objective, the firm began a major transformation to its supply chain system and the very nature of its business. The idea was to change from a local autonomy view, where each member of the supply chain optimized performance independently, to an end-to-end view, where optimization occurs across the entire business network regardless of changes in the market—creating what we have been calling the value-managed enterprise.

Central to the transformation is a national network of redistribution centers to service customers across the United States, with optimized costs associated with transportation, inventory, product handling, transactions, and fixed capital. Calling on its talented internal resources, applying many of the ingredients contained in the Wall Street Diet, and receiving advice from software provider Manhattan Associates, the objective was to optimize performance in such areas as

- strategic planning (to improve collaboration with suppliers, carriers, and customers);
- analysis and modeling (to find mutual cost-saving opportunities and optimized solutions);
- business process design (covering forecasting and fulfillment to replenishment);
- demand planning (to improve operations, warehousing, and resource and equipment planning); and
- national transportation management (to lower delivery costs while maintaining high service levels to customers).

It's a comprehensive approach that is tantamount to applying a rigorous diet across a total value network. As part of the transformation, the distributor will effectively share supply-and-demand information to optimize its total use of assets and achieve above-industry performance standards.

Manhattan's role has been to assist with the provision of best-of-breed applications in support of the vision. For example, Manhattan helped optimize the layout in many of the existing distribution centers. At the same time, Manhattan concentrated on adding value with the first planned regional distribution center. At that site, it provided a warehouse management system, a labor management program to help manage the workforce, and a performance management program as a reporting tool. Further plans call for installation of a transportation planning and execution tool and a forecasting solution.

The distributor and its suppliers, which were part of the planning of the new system, will realize savings from the change through consolidation of freight for full truckloads, minimized handling costs due to fewer product transfers, reduction in warehousing space due to more direct shipments, inventory reductions through better planning, lower transaction costs, and streamlined unloading services. Before the new system, the distributor would ship products from its suppliers to the distribution centers or directly to the operating companies. With the assistance provided by the Manhattan solutions, it now realizes savings by ordering larger volumes and maximizing outbound transportation with more full truckloads.

Customers benefit through a more effective supply chain infrastructure that will provide shorter product lead times for special orders of nonstock items, a wider variety of product availability, and consistently calculated freight rates reflecting the redistribution system. With the new system, pallet loads of mixed products can be built that are specific to customer needs. This cuts the need to break down pallets of the same product and build loads for specific shipments.

This case is just one example of how technology can enable companies to make improvements across a business enterprise. Manhattan Associates' solutions facilitate lean enterprises by coordinating activity across functional stovepipes and promoting the free flow of critical information. By providing global supply chain visibility with a common platform architecture, companies can understand actual needs, where inventory to meet those needs is at every step in the supply chain, and respond quickly to any changes in demand. This ability makes the supply chain a strategic weapon that creates competitive advantage and greater shareholder value.

SUMMARY

Our dieter needed to evaluate the new lifestyle, incorporating the new measurements and disciplines that led to the current level of success. This same approach now becomes a way to live a more fulfilling life. The plan will evolve, but its foundations remain clear.

A comprehensive approach to developing a new lifestyle will be far more effective than random or isolated efforts to improve one's health and well-being. Each new plan builds on the success of previous plans, but the individual must be ever-vigilant.

The Wall Street Diet requires a strict and rigorous business discipline, which must be integrated into the firm's strategy. It must be incorporated into the business plan and marketing plan for all segments of the business. It should contain value propositions that distinguish the network in the eyes of key customers and establish market dominance. This is how long-term revenue growth occurs.

Examples have been given to guide that determination and selection of the propositions that will differentiate the firm. The firm's future does not have to be put at risk during this exercise. Rather, we advise carefully testing the introduction and deployment of the features of the Wall Street

Diet in a controlled manner to reap the greatest benefit as the changes are absorbed across the company and its business allies, so an enhanced network becomes apparent to key customers.

CHECKLIST FOR SENIOR MANAGEMENT

☐ Strategy and strategy development are two basic responsibilities for any CEO. Create both the dreams and processes to make it effective.

☐ Encourage controlled risk taking. The risks lead to the future. The control ensures the firm will get there.

☐ Have an enormous, world-class party to celebrate the five to eight points of new profits. Include the managers, personnel and strategic partners who made it possible.

☐ Do not stop. Do not rest on your laurels.

CHECKLIST FOR FUNCTIONAL MANAGERS AND DIET CHAMPIONS

☐ Follow the strategy process outlined in the chapter to embed the Wall Street Diet into all business, operational, and marketing plans.

☐ Make sure the plans contain the value propositions that result from the diet. These will differentiate the firm and its allies from other less able and nimble competitors.

☐ Audit the strategy, plan, and results every six months to ensure that the enterprise value is being created. The top and bottom lines should show results.

AFTERWORD—GET HEALTHY

As we conclude, we want to remind you why the diet has such a broad enterprise focus. The Wall Street Diet shares a similarity with many other diets. It may be hard to get started, and it is easy to be led astray and go back to business as usual. The best advice we can give you is the same advice a physician or nutritionist would give you if you "fell off" your diet: Just start again. Often, individual dieters overindulge and give up. That is not the right approach. Our advice to you, the business dieter, is just start again. The checklists we have provided at the end of each chapter offer a way to start implementing the diet phases. In addition, they will serve as a beginning point for managers and employees.

The Wall Street Diet will prove to be controversial. It is clear that we are asking you to make substantial changes in the way your company operates—how you work with customers, suppliers, distributors, employees, and the investment community. They affect and redefine how you implement your overall business strategy. Many of your companies have launched massive programs around lean manufacturing and Six Sigma quality. It is not our intent to say that approach is wrong; it is simply not enough.

These methodologies by themselves will probably not be sufficient to bring you to optimized conditions or give you a competitive edge. Is lean bad? Is quality bad? No, it is just that a body of evidence indicates they are insufficient and, over time, lose their edge and do not become part of a corporate lifestyle. They become programs with diminishing returns. Our goal is to provide you with the tools and techniques of a rigorous and complete diet that will cause lasting change. We are proponents of taking an enterprise view, whereas many of the lean and quality initiatives we have studied limit their activities to individual plants or departments.

An example of this condition can be found in one of today's business headlines: "Delphi Declares Bankruptcy." On October 16, 2005, Delphi, an automotive industry giant, declared bankruptcy. Delphi is one of the leanest companies in existence. What does James Womack, president of the Lean Institute, have to say about Delphi?

"I have walked through dozens of Delphi facilities in many countries, and in my recent walks I have seen some of the leanest practices I have ever found outside of Toyota City. Delphi retained the very best ex-Toyota sensei, pursued kaizen and kaikaku with a vengeance, and took out billions of dollars of operating costs" (e-newsletter, October 17, 2005).

Womack is one of the foremost experts on lean manufacturing in the world. He acknowledges that Delphi is a lean leader. Yet the result was bankruptcy. Is lean wrong? No, it is not. It's a key component of the Wall Street Diet, but by itself is not enough, especially when you don't have a completely lean company and only focus on lean plants. As we prescribe in the diet, building a lean enterprise is the key. Look at the recent winners of the Shingo Prize for Excellence in Manufacturing (awarded annually to firms exemplifying lean practices), and you will see companies making impressive gains, at a plant level. Again, we think these activities are an excellent starting point, but they have to be linked to eliminating waste throughout the supply chain. You always pay for waste, whether it is on your plant floor or another's plant floor. Nor does it matter whether it's a customer or a supplier who is creating the waste. Customers will ask you for lower prices to make up for their inefficiencies, and suppliers need to make up for your inefficiencies as well as theirs.

Another point of possible contention is quality. Quality is a key component of the Wall Street Diet. Yet if we look at winners of the Malcolm Baldridge National Quality Award (given annually to U.S. businesses, sponsored by the National Institute of Technology), we see two disturbing threads: many winners are divisions or departments, the antithesis of the diet's enterprise approach, and some winners are household words, in the most dubious sense (e.g., AT&T, Lucent). The lesson on quality is clear: It has many advantages, but it must be applied broadly, not to departments or divisions—first to companies, then to enterprises. There is another lesson on quality: One size does not fit all. As quality becomes part of your new corporate lifestyle, it is important to make sure it is customized for your needs. Quality programs are about meeting customer needs and improving financial returns, not about quality per se.

The authors' view on both of these important topics is that by themselves they will not be sufficient to give you a competitive edge. Lean and quality are not bad, but they are not enough, and over time, they lose their impetus and do not become ingrained in the corporate lifestyle. Our goal is to provide you with the tools and techniques of the diet to cause lasting change—across your enterprise.

And where do we start? With the people within the enterprise! Managers and employees make up the vast majority of a company. So for an effective change in corporate lifestyle, the managers and employees must not just acknowledge the changes but wholeheartedly embrace them.

At the same time, senior management has to be in the driver's seat for the Wall Street Diet to work. For it to actually change the corporate lifestyle, the diet has to be embraced at all levels of the corporation and then extended to the entire enterprise.

The Wall Street Diet draws on successful weight loss techniques to frame the necessary actions and use terms that people will be familiar with. The first strength of the diet is facilitating communications. A simple line such as "We are putting the company on a diet" or "The company has joined a health club" will clearly communicate to all your employees, shareholders, and managers what changes are at hand. Everyone knows what it means to be on a diet or go to a health club, so one of the most critical tasks is accomplished—clear, concise communications.

The next critical task is letting people know what they can do to help. We have experienced the wait-and-see attitude from countless employees and managers as companies launch one initiative after another. Most times they are right to wait; it will likely turn out to be a short-term activity or, even worse, an unsustainable activity. But some action must be taken or the wait can become interminable.

The design of the checklists is to map the relevant chapters to concise communications and make sure you get started and lead the effort to make your company healthier. It is important to note that even the best companies can get better. And great companies can fail. So, let's all get started with the diet, and get healthy.

 APPENDIX

PARTNERING DIAGNOSTIC LABORATORY (PDL)

To assist companies in the creation of a Wall Street Diet–inspired business network or value-managed enterprise, an event is often required. Participants need to determine how to share valuable knowledge and better practices.

Proven to be extremely effective for that purpose, a *partnering diagnostic lab* (PDL) is an exercise involving multiple supply chain constituents, under the direction of a skilled facilitator and subject matter expert. PDLs focus on existing conditions and potential process improvements while setting the stage for a higher level of collaboration and results. The PDL develops mutually beneficial improvements by examining all aspects of a business relationship in areas targeted for improvement. It could encompass technical, transactional, procurement, and logistics activities. It could also encompass product, information, cash flow, and service considerations. As the overview in Exhibit A.1 indicates, a typical PDL includes an intensive search for the following elements:

- New methods and procedures that positively alter process steps in normal business activities between two or more companies
- Hidden values in supply chain network processes connecting the participants
- New processes and features of electronic communication to improve quality and shorten cycle times
- A road map toward optimized conditions in an extended enterprise that introduces cost reductions, better use of assets, and builds greater customer satisfaction and new revenues

EXHIBIT A.1 Partnering Diagnostic Lab (PDL) Overview

- **What is it?**
  A focused, facilitated, fact-supported two-day session between
  businesses to resolve how to improve
  intercompany supply chain processes

- **Who participates?**
  Appropriate representatives from
  both companies — for example:
  - Supplier: Sales/Marketing, IT, R&D
  - Customer: Purchasing, Manufacturing,
    Planning, IT, R&D

- **When is it held?**
  After preliminary discussions with both parties to
  - Identify opportunity areas
  - Define specific processes for improvement
  - Gather supporting data

- **Where is it held?**
  At the sponsor's offices or plant or a selected off-site facility

As seen in Exhibit A.2, a PDL is a two-day communication session convened between two or more businesses to improve intercompany processes and establish win-win solutions to help both entities increase performance. The secret to a successful PDL is to invite a larger cross-section of individuals than would normally be involved in intercompany discussions. Participants with fresh perspectives help analyze current process steps to discover innovative ways to address root problem causes. These participants could include sales and marketing from a supplier; purchasing, manufacturing, and planning from a customer; and information technology, and research and development from both. The idea is to broaden the scope so everyone who attends can voice an informed opinion on how a situation can be enhanced. Specific opportunities for action are defined through the chartering of improvement teams and performance measures to track benefits from changed processing.

Careful preparation at the beginning yields impressive results. A preliminary discussion conducted by the facilitator develops a current situation assessment, identifies potential areas of opportunity, defines specific processes for attention, and gathers supporting data. During this neces-

EXHIBIT A.2   Generalized Approach for Two-Day PDL Workshop

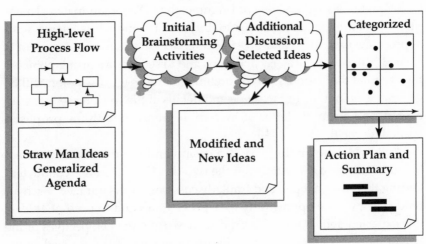

sary prediagnostic discussion, the objective is to explain the PDL procedure and develop ideas and concepts to be considered during the actual PDL. Participants agree on the framework for the discussion, which will include the following components:

- Development of process maps to describe the areas under consideration
- Consideration of best practices that could have a positive impact on the processing
- Development of ideas to achieve extra values, through
  - reduced cycle times for process completion;
  - aggregated purchasing;
  - reduced dependency on inventory and safety stocks—raw materials, work-in-process, and finished goods;
  - enhanced communications between parties, especially Internet-based linkage to improve service features;
  - better utilization of joint assets;
  - aggregated transportation opportunities; and
  - increased online visibility to supply chain process steps.

One necessary outcome of the preliminary meetings is to determine the scope, purpose, details, and deliverables from the work sessions.

Another is to specify the attendees for the PDL, making certain face-to-face conditions are possible. For example, the PDL should match IT people from both the suppliers and buyers. Through interviews with appropriate executives and possible attendees, a situation assessment is created to describe the as-is conditions and to serve as a starting point for the eventual discussion. A list of preliminary ideas for discussion will be generated, an outline of the scope and details of the working sessions accepted, and a sample letter of invitation prepared with the proposed agenda for the PDL.

Following the preliminary discussion and interviews, a site is selected, attendees are invited, and the two-day PDL session is conducted. During this session, open and frank discussions are encouraged. Each attendee is given an opportunity to express views and to present at least one expected deliverable. The process map, from the perspectives of the two or more firms represented, is discussed and agreement reached on the as-is conditions.

After considering current best practices in similar areas of processing, the facilitator moves the discussion to how the process map can be improved. Generally thirty to fifty possible improvement ideas result. The suggestions are placed in categories and breakout teams dispatched to develop specific suggestions for changes and enhancements. With help and encouragement from the facilitator and subject matter expert, a prioritized list of improvement opportunities is generated.

The final phase is to prepare specific action plans for at least five to ten of the highest-potential ideas, including team sponsor, scope of the action, required resources, action steps, timetable for completion, and order-of-magnitude costs and benefits. These actions are placed on an action grid, complete with priority ranking and timing of execution. Typical benefits achieved range between 5 and 20 percent of the involved costs, depending on the length of the relationship, the depth of current obstacles and problems, the closeness of the relationship and previous continuous improvement initiatives. Based on many PDLs, benefits could include the following:

- Reduced errors in order processing
- Savings in order fulfillment costs
  - Order to delivery
  - Order to cash
- Lower inventory

- Less warehouse space
- Reduced freight costs
- Shorter cycle times in the cash-to-cash flow
- New customer-centric metrics that drive enhanced performance
- Higher customer satisfaction ratings
- E-commerce interconnectivity features
- Communications enhancements
- New, profitable revenues

Intangible benefits derive as well:

- Better understanding of supply chain concepts and strategies
- Better understanding of operational aspects of the particular supply chain process steps
- Strengthened customer-supplier relationships
- Product rationalization
- Improved design for manufacture
- Alignment with manufacturing and materials strategies with marketplace-driven realities
- Increased partnering between IT units
- Enhanced partnering communications
- Increased knowledge of processes and applications

When the diagnostic is completed and everyone thanked for their participation, the facilitator and subject matter expert will prepare a summary of the event and issue a final report. Generally delivered within one week, this report contains a full list of all attendee expectations and whether they were met, and a list of all suggestions made and how they were synthesized into the final suggested actions. The process maps are included, as well as the situation assessment and appropriate discussion. Most important, the report includes personal views on how the action steps should be implemented and any other ideas of pertinence. Essentially, it contains the road map for implementation. Quite often, the diagnostic leads to follow-up meetings by the various action teams and periodic reports to a management review group to make certain actions are taken and the desired results are achieved.

One PDL was conducted between a major building contractor and a manufacturer of elevators leading to six teams meeting for almost a year, to completely develop the suggested actions. This session led to the major discovery that the time for completion of the elevator work could be reduced by as much as 30 percent, if the contractor gave the elevator company earlier access to the design specification and could be allowed to make alternative design suggestions. Agreement to these suggestions (much of which was accomplished electronically) not only accomplished the reduced time frame but also led to cost savings greater than 25 percent.

The cost for such diagnostics will vary according to the scope and charter, the time for the interviews required to complete the situation assessment, and the amount of necessary data available to help with the analysis and development of the final report. A reliable range is within $25,000 to $35,000.

BIBLIOGRAPHY

Aeppel, Timothy. "Manufacturers Cope with Costs of Strained Global Supply Chains." *Wall Street Journal*, December 8, 2004, A1.

Amaral, Jason, Corey Billington, and Andy Tsay. "Outsourcing Production without Losing Control." *Supply Chain Management Review*, November/December 2004, 52.

Arndt, Michael. "Why Kraft Is on a Crash Diet." *Business Week*, November 29, 2004, 46.

Bacheldor, Beth. "Ready, Set, Build." *Information Week*, June 27, 2005, 49–53.

Bowman, Robert J. "Using Supply Chain Excellence to Build Brand Reputation." *Global Logistics & Supply Chain Strategies*, August 2004, 76–79.

Cecere, Lora, Kevin O'Marah, and Laura Preslan. "Driven by Demand." *Supply Chain Management Review*, November/December 2004, 15–16.

Chabrow, Eric. "Procurement-Technology Investments Produce Big Payoffs." *Internetweek.com*, February 16, 2005.

Chandler, Clay. "Full Speed Ahead." *Fortune*, February 7, 2005, 78–84.

Chappell, Lindsay. "Big 3 Pay Price for Bad Supplier Relations." *Automotive News*, December 27, 2004.

Christopher, Martin. "Leaning into a New Landscape." *Automotive Logistics*, January/February 2005, 17.

Collins, Jim. *Good to Great: Why Some Companies Make the Leap—and Others Don't*. New York: HarperBusiness, 2001.

Duffy, Mike. "How Gillette Cleaned Up Its Supply Chain." *Supply Chain Management Review*, April 2004, 20–27.

Dutile, Robert. "Connect Demand with Supply." *CIO*, November 15, 2004.

Farrell, Diana. "Assess Your Company's Global Potential." *Harvard Business Review*, December 2004, 82–90.

Ferdows, Kasra, Michael Lewis, and Jose Machuca. "Rapid-Fire Fulfillment." *Harvard Business Review*, November 2004, 104–10.

Fiskel, Joseph, Douglas Lambert, Lee Artman, John Harris, and Hugh Share. "The New Supply Chain Edge." *Supply Chain Management Review*, July/August 2004, 50–55.

Friscia, Tony. "The $488 Billion Opportunity." *Supply Chain Management Review*, January/February 2005, 15–16.

Friscia, Tony, Kevin O'Marah, and Joe Souza. "The AMR Research Supply Chain Top 25 and the New Trillion Dollar Opportunity." Unpublished report, AMR Research, November 2004, Boston.

Fugate, Brian S., and John T. Mentzer. "Dell's Supply Chain DNA." *Supply Chain Management Review*, October 2004, 20–24.

Garvin, David A. "What Every CEO Should Know about Creating New Business." *Harvard Business Review*, July–August, 2004, 18–22.

Gottfredson, Mark, Rudy Puryear, and Stephen Phillips. "Strategic Sourcing: From Periphery to Core." *Harvard Business Review*, February 2005, 132–40.

Industry Week–Logistics Today. "Lean Six Sigma: Achieving Near-Perfection within a Lean Environment." Webcast, December 14, 2004.

Lee, Hau. "The Triple-A Supply Chain." *Harvard Business Review*, October 2004, 102–12.

Liker, Jeffrey, and Thomas Choi. "Building Deep Supplier Relationships." *Harvard Business Review*, December 2004, 104–13.

Manrodt, Karl, and Katie Vitasek. "Understanding the Lean Supply Chain." Lecture Series for Oracle Corporation, 2004.

Marcus, Gisele. "Keeping Clients, Building Business at Johnson Controls." *Velocity*, (Quarter 3 2004): 18–24.

Marlin, Steven. "Closer to Customers." *Information Week*, November 1, 2004, 81–84

McDougall, Paul. "Outsourcers Fall Short." *Information Week*, November 2004, 44–55.

Moore, Geoffrey. "Darwin and the Demon." *Harvard Business Review*, July/August 2004, 86–92.

Narayanan, V. G., and Anath Raman. "Aligning Incentives in Supply Chains." *Harvard Business Review*, November 2004, 94–102.

Nelson, David R. "How Delphi Went Lean." *Supply Chain Management Review*, November/December 2004, 32–37.

Nolan, Alexis. "The Best of Both Worlds." *Automotive Logistics*, September/October 2004, 20–26.

Poirier, Charles C. *Using Models to Improve Supply Chains*. San Francisco: Berrett-Koehler, 2003.

Pyzdek, Thomas. "Motorola's Six Sigma Program." *Qualitydigest.com*, December 1997.

Rigby, Darrell, and Dianne Ledingham. "CRM Done Fight." *Harvard Business Review*, November 2004, 118–29.

Sengupta, Sumantra. "The Top 10 Supply Chain Mistakes." *Supply Chain Management Review*, July/August 2004, 42–49.

Shingo, Shigeo. *A Revolution in Manufacturing: The SMED System*. Stamford, CT: Productivity Press, 1985.

———. "Study of Toyota Production System." Unpublished report, Japan Manufacturing Association, 1981.

Slone, Reuben E. "Leading a Supply Chain Turnaround." *Harvard Business Review*, October 2004, 114–21.

Tierney, Christine. "Good Relationships with Automakers Pay Off for Suppliers." *Detroit Free Press*, August 9, 2005, C1.

Tompkins Associates. "Lean Manufacturing." Internal supply chain excellence document M-58, www.tompkinsinc.com.

Womack, James P., Daniel T. Jones, and Daniel Roos. *The Machine That Changed the World*. New York: HarperCollins, 1990.

INDEX

189

ABOUT THE AUTHORS

Chuck Poirier is a recognized authority on supply chain management, process improvement, e-business techniques, and collaborative use of technology around the world. He has authored or coauthored twelve business books, seven of which have been related to improving supply chain processing. His work has been translated into nine languages. He is a frequent presenter at national and international conferences and meetings. With more than forty years' business experience, including senior-level positions, and the extensive research conducted for the writing of his many books, white papers, and position documents, Poirier is comfortable before any audience seeking help with value chain networks. He has helped firms in a variety of industries establish the framework for their supply chains and find the hidden values across the collaborative networking that can be established. His advanced techniques have become a hallmark of firms seeking the most benefits from cross-organizational collaboration.

Mike Bauer has breadth and depth that are unique in today's compartmentalized business world. He is a noted author and speaker, whose "hands-on" approach differentiates him from many others in the world of business and technology expertise. Bauer is characterized by tireless energy, boundless curiosity, and the ability to understand how business and technology trends converge. He is as comfortable on a plant floor as he is in a board room. Bauer has spoken and written on a broad range of topics, from supply chain to lean manufacturing. He is the director of Computer Sciences Corporation's Lean Enterprise Center and is a CSC Six Sigma champion.

Bauer is considered by his peers to be one of the world's leading experts on process improvement and the development and deployment of extended supply chains. He has authored two books, written articles, given speeches, and worked with companies around the world, streamlining business processes and linking customers and suppliers into seamless and successful business networks. His recent work focuses on achieving superior business results via supply chain excellence.

Bill Houser, president of Integrated Productivity and Quality Systems, Inc., has a lengthy history helping businesses improve performance and enhance profitability. He has trained hundreds of business professionals in the principles of world-class quality and productivity. Houser has worked with more than one hundred corporations and government agencies in the United States, Canada, Mexico, and Europe. He is the coauthor of *Business Partnering for Continuous Improvement* and has written numerous articles on quality, productivity, and cost improvement. His models for success have stood the test of time and implementation and are considered valuable aids in the fight against corporate obesity.

ABOUT
BERRETT-KOEHLER PUBLISHERS

Berrett-Koehler is an independent publisher dedicated to an ambitious mission: Creating a World that Works for All.

We believe that to truly create a better world, action is needed at all levels—individual, organizational, and societal. At the individual level, our publications help people align their lives and work with their deepest values. At the organizational level, our publications promote progressive leadership and management practices, socially responsible approaches to business, and humane and effective organizations. At the societal level, our publications advance social and economic justice, shared prosperity, sustainable development, and new solutions to national and global issues. We publish groundbreaking books focused on each of these levels. To further advance our commitment to positive change at the societal level, we have recently expanded our line of books in this area and are calling this expanded line "BK Currents."

A major theme of our publications is "Opening Up New Space." They challenge conventional thinking, introduce new points of view, and offer new alternatives for change. Their common quest is changing the underlying beliefs, mindsets, institutions, and structures that keep generating the same cycles of problems, no matter who our leaders are or what improvement programs we adopt.

We strive to practice what we preach—to operate our publishing company in line with the ideas in our books. At the core of our approach is stewardship, which we define as a deep sense of responsibility to administer the company for the benefit of all of our "stakeholder" groups: authors, customers, employees, investors, service providers, and the communities and environment around us. We seek to establish a partnering relationship with each stakeholder that is open, equitable, and collaborative.

We are gratified that thousands of readers, authors, and other friends of the company consider themselves to be part of the "BK Community." We hope that you, too, will join our community and connect with us through the ways described on our website at www.bkconnection.com.

BE CONNECTED

Visit Our Website

Go to www.bkconnection.com to read exclusive previews and excerpts of new books, find detailed information on all Berrett-Koehler titles and authors, browse subject-area libraries of books, and get special discounts.

Subscribe to Our Free E-Newsletter

Be the first to hear about new publications, special discount offers, exclusive articles, news about bestsellers, and more! Get on the list for our free e-newsletter by going to www.bkconnection.com.

Participate in the Discussion

To see what others are saying about our books and post your own thoughts, check out our blogs at www.bkblogs.com.

Get Quantity Discounts

Berrett-Koehler books are available at quantity discounts for orders of ten or more copies. Please call us toll-free at (800) 929-2929 or email us at bkp.orders@aidcvt.com.

Host a Reading Group

For tips on how to form and carry on a book reading group in your workplace or community, see our website at www.bkconnection.com.

Join the BK Community

Thousands of readers of our books have become part of the "BK Community" by participating in events featuring our authors, reviewing draft manuscripts of forthcoming books, spreading the word about their favorite books, and supporting our publishing program in other ways. If you would like to join the BK Community, please contact us at bkcommunity@bkpub.com.